REIKI HEALING
FOR THE CHAKRAS

REIKI

HEALING FOR THE

CHAKRAS

TECHNIQUES TO BALANCE YOUR
MIND, BODY, AND SPIRIT

APRIL PFENDER

**ROCKRIDGE
PRESS**

Interior and Cover Designer: Gabe Nansen
Art Producer: Melissa Malinowksy
Editor: Jesse Aylen
Production Editor: Dylan Julian
Production Manager: Jose Olivera

All illustrations used under license from Shutterstock

Paperback ISBN: 978-1-63807-124-2
eBook ISBN: 978-1-63807-583-7
R0

~~~~~~~

TO ALL OF MY BELOVED STUDENTS,
who have shown curiosity and dedication
to their own expansion. May this work
bless your journey of awakening and may it
serve you as well as everyone you
touch in your service work.

TO MY BELOVED WILL,
thank you for being my heartbeat.
In gratitude always, April.

~~~~~~~

CONTENTS

INTRODUCTION
The world of energy sparked my interest at a young age.

I found myself naturally intuitive, curious about crystals and the way plants seemed to speak to me personally, and I spent endless hours outside, basking in the sun or playing in the forest. Maybe the same was true for you. Our inherent connection to the natural world has a way of plugging us directly back into ourselves—allowing us to experience our energy intimately in new and undiscovered ways.

Reiki is much the same way. This ancient modality is a pathway to accessing greater healing for your mind, body, and soul. It allows us to access simple ways to restore health and vitality and rediscover our inherent power to heal from within. The ability to channel energy and create positive impacts for the benefit of others as well as ourselves is exciting and remarkable, and I'm so thankful that you've chosen to embark on this beautiful, life-changing path.

Along the way, winding ourselves into this beautiful healing modality of Reiki, we'll explore the chakras in depth and help clarify why working within the chakra system is complementary to a Reiki practice. *Chakra* (a Sanskrit word) as a concept was passed down through many cultures all over the ancient world, with a main contributor being Hinduism. These "wheels of light" extend in vortex spirals behind and in front of the body and govern the physical and emotional functions you experience. Reiki and the chakras may stem from different traditions, but in this practice, they blend together well in a consensual communion.

As a Reiki Master Teacher (RMT), it is my life's work and mission to assist others in their personal healing journeys so that they may empower themselves through this practice. After all, a true healer doesn't "heal" you; rather, they help hold the energetic space in which you heal yourself. I've led thousands of students on their personal energy healing journeys and seen just as many life-altering transformations through this work over the years. Some may even call these radical shifts "miracles." Many of those students now have a great number of their own RMT students who have trained with them. My past three books have served the conscious community in learning more about chakras and healing in general. As an educator, it's my great honor to share this energy with you and be here to help inspire your journey into the world of energy medicine.

For me, Reiki was always a particularly inviting field of interest. I found that all healing comes in waves and really finds you exactly when you need it. My exploration of chakras initially came at a time of great healing for my mind and body, when I was hungry to learn ways to naturally heal myself both physically and emotionally. I found that by learning to balance my chakras, my energy levels became sustainable so I could work a long day without feeling drained. My heart was more open, and I was opening doors in my life where there once were walls. My life changed for the better, permanently.

This book walks you through how to use Reiki to heal and balance the chakras to achieve personal and spiritual growth. The material presented here is perfect for beginning healing practitioners to both build knowledge of the chakra system and learn about Reiki techniques and traditions. I discuss what each of these are and how they work together to complement an energy medicine or holistic healing practice. Use the guidance in this book from start to finish (recommended for beginners) or navigate to the chapter you are interested in. This book has a flexible structure to allow you to choose what you need in the moment, without feeling lost if you tend to skip around.

It is my hope that this knowledge will inspire you to use your connection to Reiki, your Reiki channel, to improve your life and expand spiritually with grace, ease, and confidence. With a dedicated practice, and some time and effort spent using your gifts and connecting to Spirit, anyone can learn this practical modality. The science of quantum physics has acknowledged the presence of a unifying force of energy between all matter in the Universe. This life force unites the body, mind, and Spirit with Source energy. Therefore, Reiki can be used to experience oneness with all that is.

Through this work, you'll be able to provide a healing space for yourself or to help people heal themselves in profound ways. Whether you plan on using Reiki for your own health and wellness, or you plan on expanding your practice into Reiki Master Teacher training, this book is a great starting point. I wish you many blessings of love and light through this time of awakening. May your application and integration of this work be a joy and an illumination in your life.

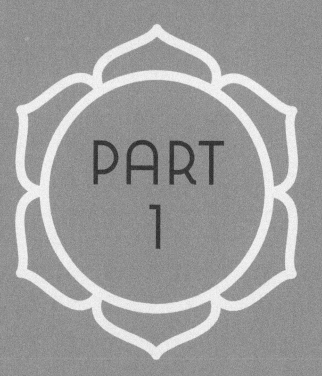

PART
1

REIKI-CHAKRA CONNECTION

We begin our Reiki-chakra journey covering many foundational aspects to build your general knowledge of both the Reiki practice and the Reiki-chakra connection. This part explains what the chakras are and how they influence our emotions, body, and mind. We explore the energetic nature of everything around us and begin to see how it ties into our own divine human nature.

By the end, you'll have a firm handle on all the foundational elements of Reiki practice. We touch on the practice itself and how it works, and review the traditional Reiki symbols. You will be introduced to a variety of techniques you can easily use to help heal yourself and others. When you choose to work with Reiki, you choose a path of working with divine light consciousness to help transmute any darkness or negativities within and around you. Bless your journey, lightworker!

~~~~

CHAPTER 1

THE CHAKRAS

Welcome to the world of energy healing. As you learn about Reiki, a valuable modality birthed from Eastern healing traditions, you'll also be guided through the Reiki-chakra connection. Key to understanding this connection is how energy relates to the physical and non-physical self, and learning to interact with this energy to effect healing.

This chapter dives into the nature of energy and how it impacts and influences our lives. It explores the human biofield or aura, followed by a look into the portals of energy we call the chakras. You'll learn what the chakras are, how they influence our physical bodies and emotions, and what it means when our chakras are blocked, versus when they're balanced. Finally, it touches on your ability to heal your chakras through a variety of common healing modalities.

ENERGY EVERYWHERE

The word *Reiki* refers to the "universal energy" that exists within all things (*rei* meaning "Universe," *ki* meaning "energy"). Universal energy composes the fabric of our existence as well as the material world and everything operating within it. Energy flows in and around absolutely everything. Looking at the world around us, we can see and touch the denser physical objects—like a car or chair. We tend to feel or sense the less dense energies rather than see them with our eyes. Examples include emotions, temperatures, or fragrances. Everything carries its own unique energetic pattern or frequency signature. In fact, physical and non-physical matter are just two forms of the same thing, vibrating or oscillating at different frequencies. These distinguishing factors are how we can naturally tell things apart and pick up on all the subtle nuances defining one experience or sensation from another. Every living being, including humans, has a unique vibratory signature, much like individual fingerprints or genetic coding.

This universal, life-sustaining energy is known as *ki* (Japanese) or *chi* (Chinese) in Eastern medicine. This is the *prana*, or essential life-force energy, that moves through everything. All living organisms carry prana. From the food we eat, the trees growing in the yard, the water flowing in the stream, to animals and human beings; we are all part of the larger body of energy that comprises this reality. Subtle energies move through us, animating our bodies, facilitating breath, and allowing us to feel our emotional states. These energies move in and out of the body via the chakra system.

Before we get into what exactly the chakras are, it's important to understand the different layers comprising your energy body and your physical body vessel. Just beyond your physical body exists your auric field. There are seven layers to your aura, and your aura contains your chakras. Each auric layer corresponds to a chakra center on the body. Both your aura and your chakras comprise your energy field, and the energy fields of all living things. It's these layers that respond to human thought and feeling, which can grow or shrink the field. Mainly, your aura (also called your biofield or etheric template) is responsible for sensing energies around you and regulating your personal magnetics. Certain layers are even responsible for downloading higher levels of intangible information into your physical body.

Think of these layers as blankets covering your body and moving out in rings all around it. It surprises many people, including some of my Reiki students, that the size of the human aura can be quite large. On average, auras can range anywhere from three to six feet wide, and, on the larger side, up to sixty feet wide! It's also possible to throw your aura to the front or to the back of your energy body if you are feeling threatened or endangered; likewise, it expands when we feel excited, safe, and loved.

Although it takes lots of practice to start to visually sense the aura with the third eye (seeing the aura), it can be sensed with the hands with a simple technique called a body scan. This practice is something I teach to my level 1 students, and it's pretty easy to practice on another person. You start from the other side of the room and gently move toward the other person until you feel a slight change in energy or pushback. This marks the edges of the biofield. You may ask the person to think happy thoughts and remeasure to note how the size and feel of the aura changes. You can also stand within the aura and sweep your hands along the body, noting any temperature changes or physical sensations for feedback. You can also use a dowsing rod or create a DIY rod from an old coat hanger. Try it out—you'll have fun reading auras in no time!

CHAKRAS EXPLAINED

Now that we've talked about the layers of the energy and physical bodies, let's explore chakras. We know that everything in existence is made of energy, which means everything has a vibration or frequency. The human body is no exception. On, above, and around the body exist energy centers that govern the energy entering or leaving the body at any given time. Think of these as invisible doorways that allow energy to pass in and out. These energy centers are considered either transpersonal, subpersonal, or corporeal, meaning they are above, below, or atop the physical body. They correspond to different body systems, organs, glands, and functions, and some even share chakras across multiple systems. In the ancient Hindu tradition, the word *chakra* translates roughly to "wheel of light." Each wheel is projected in front of and behind a person's physical body and has a spin to it, whirling open or closed when it gains or loses energy.

We'll touch on how to tell the difference among chakras, as well as what specific areas each chakra represents, in the upcoming sections of this book. For now, it's enough to understand that these portals or vortexes are actually areas of intersecting energy points that connect inward. We can't see them with the naked eye, but we can feel that they are real because we can sense the direct effects they have on the body. For example, a closed throat chakra will create certain symptoms that register on a physical level, like a sore throat, stiff neck, inability to communicate or express clear opinions, or jaw pain. Some of these issues may take time to show up, and some may present as being non-physical (such as feeling unheard or misunderstood).

Since our system is holistic, everything is connected and has an influence on the other parts of the whole. When all the chakras are open, aligned, and balanced, the energy body is running optimally and functions properly. Your body will feel healthy and you'll be able to stay present and even-keeled with your emotions. It is possible to feel the direct influence on the body and emotions as this subtle energy can impact us within hours or days. Some more serious issues, illnesses, and diagnoses may take years to accumulate in the system until they present as physical symptoms, which is why it is important to purify and cleanse the energy system regularly.

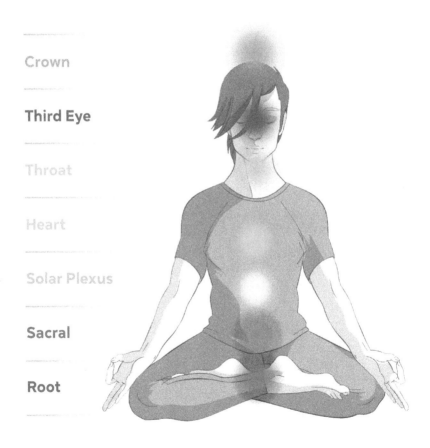

Crown

Third Eye

Throat

Heart

Solar Plexus

Sacral

Root

In this book, we'll touch on the seven main energy centers: the crown, third eye, throat, heart, solar plexus, sacral, and root chakras. These are considered the primary corporeal chakras as they lie atop and correspond to areas on the physical body. My book *The Complete Guide to Chakras: Activating the 12-Chakra Energy System for Balance and Healing* looks at all the energy centers on and alongside the body. This current book touches on everything you need to know as a beginner to Reiki and chakras, and if you seek more advanced theory and information, feel free to reference *The Complete Guide to Chakras*.

There also exist within the energy system minor chakra points, meridians, and nadis. We will touch on the main minor chakra points in this book, but keep in mind, in some cultures there are hundreds (up to 365!) of smaller chakra points on the body. It's not necessary to work with all of these individually, especially since Reiki is an intelligent energy and knows where to go once you direct it with your intention. Here, it is important to note two other important energy channels that exist within the body: the meridians and nadis.

In TCM (traditional Chinese medicine), meridian lines run like a superhighway connecting specific acupressure points on the body. We have 14 main meridian lines, and most of them run through the seven main chakras. Then there are the *nadis*, meaning "tube" or "channel," which are the two primary energy channels that run up and down the body. These are the *ida* and *pingala* lines, which are often seen as relating directly to the two main hemispheres of the brain in terms of how they function and behave.

When starting to learn about Reiki, the chakra method covers all the bases, as the chakras also include these other smaller energy lines and pathways. Focusing attention and mindfulness to your chakras helps create positive space for healing to occur. When you start to address your energy, you have the ability to decrease stress levels, end trauma and negative thinking cycles, and restore balance to your body, mind, and Spirit.

Kundalini Energy

Another form of energy that exists within the body is called *kundalini* or Shakti energy. Kundalini is known as "the coiled serpent" in Sanskrit and its roots lie in ancient practices of Hindu, Tibetan, and other Eastern cultures. This serpentine energy is thought to wind its way up the spinal column (an ascending energy), whereas Reiki is a descending energy (moving down the spine from crown to root).

Kundalini energy typically lies dormant and can be awakened during the course of a person's life in various ways. Once the kundalini energy ascends up the spine and reaches the crown, having been activated through a process called *shaktipat*, enlightenment will be achieved, as there will be no more karma to work through in that lifetime. This awakening process can give rise to higher levels of consciousness.

Although it is not essential to work on awakening the kundalini energy, many energy practitioners enjoy the work, as it can definitely enhance the quality of energy experienced and is the next step in the mastery of one's own energy. Sometimes it is possible to receive a partial or full kundalini awakening from a Reiki attunement or other energetic practice that feels activational in nature. You can tell your kundalini energy has started to move if you are experiencing heightened sensual (tantric) states of being, are feeling more sensitive to energy in general, and feel a warm energetic sensation consistently moving up your spine.

A BALANCING ACT

In order to feel healthy and energetic, as well as physically, emotionally, and spiritually fit, it's important to keep your chakras well-balanced. Because we can't see our chakras, it may not be apparent when we are blocked or off-balance, but we can feel when this happens. If you've ever struggled with your emotional state, your motivation, weight gain or loss, control issues, interpersonal relationships, or your sex drive, you know what it feels like to feel "off." And that's okay—everyone feels like this from time to time, and it usually takes several things to throw us off in a big way. We are creatures of habit, which means that we tend to repeatedly place our energy in the same energetic spots. This eventually leads to blockages if the energy isn't moved or cleared naturally. Fortunately, there are ways you can manage this balancing act to ensure you don't fall victim to your own habits and tendencies.

Balanced and open chakras contribute to a fully stabilized energy system in the body. They work together in unison to create health and harmony. Your chakras are constantly working for you by upshifting and downshifting vibrations in and out between your physical and non-physical layers. When they are fully balanced, they are uniform in their spin (much like whirlpools), size, and shape (although we can't see them).

Luckily for us, the body wants to stay in balance—that's its natural proclivity. When there are barriers to balance, it's normally because we are disowning that part of us that believes we're in charge of our reality. For example, your body feeds you impulses intuitively all day: what to eat, whom to interact with, when to rest. It's up to us to start to listen so that we can create the changes our energy is asking for. Identifying any issues that stand in your way is your first step; then you can implement a plan of action to regain balance in your life on all levels.

To get your chakras to perform properly and stay open, the entire system, as well as each chakra, needs your attention and time. Just as you shouldn't expect to work out at the gym once and stay fit for the rest of your life, you shouldn't expect one meditation or one nutritious meal to solve a lifetime of poor habits. New habits take at least 21 days to form, and some of these are easier to accomplish than you may think.

Having read and reread the energy week after week of individuals who have steadily shown improvements to their overall energy and have brought balance to all areas of their lives, I've seen that the top contributing behaviors include: meditating on a regular basis (including visualization meditations), eating healthily, having an open heart and mind, making time for rest and repair, and adopting and practicing regular energy-moving techniques. Techniques like these are crucial in helping build a powerful self-love practice that complements the mind, body, and Spirit and creates immense spiritual growth. With these changes in place, you'll be creating a resonance and coherence in your environment and interactions that continuously reflect a harmonious vibration back to you. By modifying the energies you put out with a positive attitude and commitment to your own growth, you'll be on your way to cultivating the changes you want to see. Remember to take things at your own pace so that you have plenty of time to integrate the changes required for optimal balance.

UNDERPERFORMING CHAKRAS

On occasion, your chakras may become blocked or fall out of balance. The terms *alignment* and *balance* are interchangeable here when discussing chakra health. In general, an off-balance chakra doesn't necessarily mean there is a blockage, but it can. When you are feeling that something is "off," it is usually an indication of an imbalance, whereas if you are experiencing noticeable physical or emotional changes, it's likely that you're experiencing a blockage. Confused as to which is which? Let's break it down a bit further so it's easy to understand.

No one wants an underperforming chakra, but it's natural and it happens. It's really nothing to stress about, and it can be easily restored back to an open and balanced state. You see, over time, all living beings store tensions, stressors, traumas, and excess emotional energies in the physical body as well as in the non-physical auric space. This can happen with painful, low-vibrating emotions like sadness or anger, or when we get hung up on something and feel unable to move on. We put these energies away and store them in the same place until the energies accumulate and become congested. Once that happens, we may experience dysfunction on a physical, emotional, or spiritual level. We call this state *dis-ease* because it is a state of being out-of-ease. Sometimes that means becoming ill or going through a purge process. Other times, it is more of an emotional effect, which can manifest as irritability, sadness, or strife.

When the energy is no longer able to move freely through a chakra, the chakra is blocked. If the energy is slow-moving but still able to move, the chakra is experiencing imbalance. It will generally be at a lower vibration than the other chakras because its speed and frequency are slower and lower, and the shape of the chakra may be atypical. If the chakra is imbalanced, chances are it is also out of alignment. I use these two terms interchangeably during the course of my practice.

Telling the difference between a blockage and an imbalance can seem tricky if you aren't experienced with reading chakras, but this basic level 1 Reiki skill becomes easier, especially with practice. Even without an attunement, you could learn to read your chakras with a pendulum to determine if they are blocked or out of balance. You can use anything as a pendulum (a necklace works well) and just ask simple "yes" and "no" questions to determine the health or status of an open or closed chakra.

Know that blockages and imbalances are not the same as energetic cords or attachments, which can also reside in the chakras. Energy cords are lines of energy between a person and another person, a person and a place, or a person and thing that are subconsciously siphoning energy away from the person. Both unhealthy and healthy cords can exist. For example, you may have an unhealthy cord tying you to an old lover whom you'd rather forget, or you may have a healthy cord tying you to your new niece whom you wish you could visit more often. Similarly, attachments, which are disembodied energies that like to stick around the body, can also be both unhealthy and healthy. They appear when your vibrational field is low, and they can be easily cleansed with Reiki energy.

HEALING CHAKRAS

For the past decade and then some, I have been practicing chakra healing work. The concept is simple: We can work with our own energy flow to help restore it to the optimal vibration. A high vibrational state allows us to continue to function the way we want to in the world. This state allows us to attract our desires, manifest opportunities and new blessings, boost our mood, and achieve a state of holistic wellness. When our energy systems feel off, it's just a matter of noticing and then taking inspired action to restore health and happiness.

Let's discuss some common energy healing practices I've seen work for my clients in the past: sound healing, space clearing, essential oils, meditation, and Reiki. You can try to implement these techniques in your own practice, or regular daily or monthly rituals to help in your own healing. The most common and easiest way to boost your mood is to add high vibrations to your life!

First up is working with sound healing. Sound is an easy way to change your vibes quickly and effortlessly. If you don't have access to a studio that has sound-bath offerings, there are plenty of offerings online (both paid and free). Start by selecting music to listen to that boosts your mood (like brain-entrainment tones or meditative soundtracks) and add some healing crystals or Tibetan bowls, chimes, or gongs. Put them on in the background when doing chores, working, or before you fall asleep at night.

Next, you might try to give your living and working spaces an energy makeover. Declutter—throw out the old items collecting dust and holding old memories or stories, and remove any items that aren't complementing your lifestyle anymore. Saying goodbye feels healthy and will actually boost your energy. Close a chapter of your life by moving items out of your space. Afterward, try adding some friendly, inspiring new art and some high-frequency crystals to bring in exactly the energy you want. I love working with amethyst (for intuition), rose quartz (for heart healing), clear quartz (for energy boosting), and selenite (for clearing old energies). They are regulars around my home and workspace. You can even pop these in your to-go bag, pockets, or bra to infuse your day with crystal healing and gain some added chakra support.

Essential oils are next on the list, as these scents awaken the senses and directly impact the limbic system. The limbic system is responsible for regulating important automatic functions in the body, like metabolism, heart rate, breathing, stress levels, and more. If you want to calm yourself quickly and drop into instant relaxation, these oils derived from natural plant extracts work directly on your body's natural physiological responses.

One of the most significant methods I've seen affect someone's healing capability is the willingness to pick up a meditation practice. Meditation isn't about eliminating all thoughts from your mind. Rather, it is about learning to surf the waves of emotions and thoughts that clutter your mental space all day. Eventually, you may find that a regular practice helps you achieve stillness more quickly, but the point is to take time each day to sit with your own energy and mind. Visualization meditations can assist in powerful healings when you are working with a physical issue or illness, and I've seen them work miracles in the world of healing.

Finally, Reiki is a time-honored healing tradition that I always suggest to clients who are ready to take the plunge and energetically "reset." This is a simple practice that will clear any blockages within the aura, chakra system, and physical body so that your energy is able to flow freely again. I like to describe it as acupuncture without the needles.

Reiki changed my life and it can change yours, too. Are you ready?

CHAPTER 2

REIKI HEALING

This chapter focuses on the different levels of Reiki and what transpires at each. I also provide a brief overview of symbols commonly used in Reiki so that you gain some exposure to the shortcuts Reiki uses to access energy. My aim is that you'll discover exactly how Reiki works, which will illuminate the importance of your direct relationship to Source to strengthen your spiritual practice.

What follows is an introduction to Reiki energy healing and an exploration of what Reiki is and how it began. I include other parts of Reiki history that are particularly relevant to modern-day teachings. Specifically, we will look at how Reiki can heal and we will cover the big questions. Together, we review the Three Pillars and Five Principles of Usui Reiki, and I provide some Reiki techniques for beginners to the practice. These techniques vary by level of Reiki attunement, which we explore further as we move through the chapters in this book.

REIKI 101

Reiki is a spiritual practice as well as a healing modality and will awaken you to new layers of awareness and your inherent abilities. There are many paths to healing, and Reiki will aid you in your spiritual development as you cultivate a practice that's just right for you. It is both a self-healing tool and a tool to help heal others (both locally and remotely, from a distance). By letting your heart guide you, you will be able to use this energy safely, gently, and effectively to realize great change on all levels—physical, emotional, mental, and spiritual. All the practice requires is a sense of surrender, a necessary part of the spiritual path—giving up your desire to control everything. With Reiki, you will be better able to allow the loving frequencies of the Universe to flow through you abundantly, without resistance.

The name *Reiki* comprises two words—*rei* meaning "Universal," and *ki* meaning "energy." It's more easily interpreted to mean spiritual consciousness, or energy from Source. You don't have to be religious to appreciate, receive, enjoy, or practice Reiki. Many practices incorporate the movement of *ki* through the physical body as a means of healing (such as acupuncture, chi gong, and tai chi). Remember, *ki* is life-force energy that permeates all things (also known as prana). The science of quantum physics has acknowledged the presence of this unifying force of energy among all matter in the Universe. Therefore, Reiki can be used to experience oneness with all that is.

Reiki has been practiced since before recorded history. We see evidence of it in Egyptian art renderings and again in the mystery schools of the ancient world, and Reiki has since come to see its day again in modern-day Japan and across the West. Although it's primarily an Eastern healing practice, Reiki is used by practitioners worldwide. There are many lineages of Reiki practice throughout various cultures, but the most common is called Usui Reiki.

Dr. Mikao Usui was responsible for opening the first Reiki healing practice in 1921 in Tokyo, Japan. As a Buddhist monk with a background in theology and philosophy, he was inspired to seek a way to heal himself and others. He spent years developing the method after a spiritual download he received while meditating on Mount Kurama for 21 days. He founded the Reiki Method of Healing (Usui Shiki Ryoho) after years of spiritual cultivation and took on only 11 master students.

Two such practitioners, Dr. Chujiro Hayashi and Madam Hawayo Takata, were later responsible for establishing Reiki as a holistic healing modality that would then be spread to a wider audience than ever before imagined. Dr. Hayashi helped develop the hand placements specific to Usui Reiki, and Madam Takata later brought this lineage to the Western world via Hawaii. Through Reiki, the West has adopted new ways to treat the cause, not the effect, of illness. Reiki has been able to flourish, bringing people back into the ways of natural healing.

THE THREE PILLARS

In his teachings, Dr. Usui passed on the foundations, or pillars, of Reiki to each of his practitioners. These pillars—gassho, reiji-ho, and chiryo—each have their own role and serve multiple purposes. Dr. Usui created this specific format of Reiki to enable anyone to engage in the flow of healing without draining their own vital life force. The pillars set up a safe container in which to practice and give general guidelines for the natural healing system. Let's look at each individually.

Gassho, the first pillar of Reiki, is a meditative practice and offers the element of spiritual hygiene. Gassho is to be performed after you have set up your healing space and, if you're practicing on another person, have chatted with them to determine the focus of the session. The concept is simple—the hands come together in a prayer position. As you do this, your focus should be on centering and breathing into the heart space—the area including your heart and the etheric space around your heart where your emotions are held. This is an excellent way to energetically clear yourself and the space you are working in to ensure clarity and calm prior to performing treatment. You should do this before every session for 5 to 10 minutes or more, as you should never enter a session with a cluttered mind or heart. Focus on the breath and exhale any tensions that need to be released in order to be completely present. You may also move back into gassho at the completion of a session in order to ground yourself.

The second pillar of Reiki is known as reiji-ho. With this pillar, you set intentions around the healing about to take place. This is a critical part of the process, not to be skipped. The mind and power of affirmations are powerful, and during reiji-ho, we speak our intentions into existence. This is also a time to call in guidance and ask directly for assistance. When you are opening up to Reiki energy, you are establishing your spiritual channel. This is the perfect opportunity to get quiet and begin to notice the subtle information you are picking up about the person you are working on. This part of your practice requires trust, mindfulness, and an open mind. Once you receive guidance, intend for the Reiki energy to work for the greatest good, within the most beneficial timeline for you or your patient.

The last pillar of Reiki is the chiryo, or "treatment." There's no wrong way to do this if you've spent time preparing yourself and setting your intentions appropriately, although it is recommended to keep your legs uncrossed during a Reiki transmission so that it does not negatively impact the flow of the energy. When you begin your treatment, most practitioners will use the chakra method (described in this book) because it covers the entire body, head to toe. The movements may seem to go in a specific order, and the practitioner trusts that the energy is reaching all the places it needs to go. Hold each hand position for approximately three to five minutes or until your intuition guides you to move on or stop the session. Most full treatments are between 45 and 55 minutes in length, so give yourself plenty of time to work without feeling rushed.

The Five Principles

Dr. Usui believed that the Reiki principles were a form of spiritual practice. As part of his practice, he recommended observing these principles, as well as meditating on them daily and incorporating them into a practice (much like a dojo). By taking each day one at a time, we live in the moment. Thus, the original principles state that they are "the secret method of inviting blessings, the spiritual medicine of many illnesses." They each begin with the statement "Just for today," meaning that today we have a choice that is unattached to yesterday or tomorrow. Everything is temporary; life is constantly changing, and we get to decide if we will truly allow it to be witnessed so it can be released.

Here are the principles in their entirety:

Just for today, I will not worry.
... I will not be angry.
... I will do my work honestly.
... I will give thanks to my many blessings.
... I will be kind to my neighbor and all living things.

Worry brings us into the past or future and away from the present moment. Anger, although functional, as it serves to indicate when something is out of alignment or needs attention, is generally a lower vibrational energy and not something we need to live in to understand the lessons it may teach. Doing our work with integrity reminds us of how to stay in alignment throughout the day.

HEALING POWER

I have personally seen the power of Reiki effect many healings, including releasing anxiety and stress and restoring physical and mental well-being. Reiki can also be used to charge water, food, crystals, plants, animals, and children. Infusing something with Reiki energy boosts it with high-vibrational energy that will keep working on dissolving the lower, denser energies, creating a healing effect. This is called *entrainment*, and it's the process of transmuting or changing energy to a higher state. This happens when a lower-vibrating object syncs with a higher-vibrating object, converting the dense energy waves into lighter particles with a higher frequency.

The way Reiki healing works is simple. The practitioner directs universal energy through their hands into the body and energetic field of the recipient receiving treatment. Depending on the permission granted and the desired method of treatment, the practitioner will place their hands directly on the patient's physical body or will stay within their aura (without physical touch) to perform the treatment. There are pros to each method, and you'll need to explore the practice to determine which method is right for you and the recipient.

Perhaps what is most inspiring about Reiki energy is that there's no incorrect way to use it. Reiki has its own intelligence and consciousness, as the nature of the energy is the same that flows in and around everything—it is universal and divine. As such, the direction the energy flows from Source (above the head or crown area) is down and out through the practitioner's hands. This noninvasive energy flows easily through the body channel, and this energy can be felt by both the practitioner and the recipient. The spinal channel is opened during a process called *attunement*, which only takes a few minutes and can be done in person or remotely.

Anyone can do Reiki, and chances are you have already done some form of Reiki in the past without even knowing it. With an attunement, you will be able to channel Reiki without feeling depleted. An attunement is a sacred rite of passing on the Reiki symbols from master to student practitioner. During an attunement, the aura is opened, and the symbols are entered into the crown and the palms of the student. This energy is then absorbed, through intention, into the field and body of the practitioner. This absorption can be experienced as energy fluctuations, shifting lights, body temperature changes, and feeling "lighter" as the energy begins to open the spinal channel. It will continue its work for the next 21 days, as a cleanse begins and the physical, mental, and spiritual states start to purify and open. We'll get into that later in this chapter after we discuss the different levels of Reiki (see "Reiki for Chakra Healing," page 33).

An attunement is required to progress to each subsequent level of practice and allows the practitioner to be able to channel Reiki themselves. It is different from having a session in which the practitioner is simply receiving the energy transmission during a treatment. Attunements are also recommended for people who are healing serious illness or chronic conditions, as they will then be able to move more energy through the open spinal channel and give themselves self-healing on a daily basis. If you fall into this category, consider an attunement to level 1 to aid in your ongoing journey.

Most people are natural healers. They, like you, were born with easy access to healing abilities and often appear to intuitively channel the most beneficial energy for someone in need. However, keep in mind that any form of healing requires training and experience. Once you are attuned, you can channel Reiki energy for self-healing or to help heal others. The healing can be used to soften past timelines, send healing to future events, promote good health, and work on people not physically present with you during a remote session.

Importantly, Reiki is not a substitute for receiving medical treatment when needed. As a practitioner, never recommend going against a doctor's advice, especially if there is a known medical condition. This can be tempting when someone comes in and wishes to take themselves off medications, but unless you are a medical doctor or are working directly with the patient's doctor with written consent, this is unwise. The world of natural medicine often encourages intuitive, holistic advice, so use a patient-treatment consent form if you are seeing clients on a regular basis, and stay within approved guidelines.

21-DAY CLEANSE

Each time a practitioner receives an attunement (initiation) for any level of Reiki, a cleansing experience follows. This process helps naturally purify the chakras and affects the physical, emotional, mental, and spiritual layers of the self. This period of cleansing may also be called a detoxification, because there is a distinct shedding of layers as the old, stagnant energies are pushed out of the system. Receiving an attunement amplifies higher vibrational energies, leaving very little room for lower vibrations such as disease, illness, anger, or anxiety to exist in the same space in the body.

During the cleanse, each chakra is purified over a course of about three days. Sometimes it's possible to feel the energy working through a specific chakra or in multiple chakras at once. There is no particular order but, in general, the energies will begin clearing through the lower vibrations first, which means if you have blockages in certain areas, those will be addressed early on.

Though this doesn't happen often, it's possible to experience what is known as a "healing crisis" while someone's energy is going through any type of cleanse (including a regular session, not just attunements). A healing crisis in natural medicine is a brief and temporary period during which symptoms seem to worsen before they get better. For example, you may experience seasonal allergies; therefore, in a healing crisis, they may flare up into congestion before they subside entirely. A healing crisis is typically short and can be identified as such only after the effects have eased. With this knowledge, you'll be able to recognize this period as beneficial to overall healing and retain a sense of well-being, despite momentary discomfort.

Since this energy upgrade ushers in a detoxification process, it's wise to follow some basic self-care practices during this time. Getting regular exercise or incorporating a movement practice (yoga, Pilates, jogging, stretching) will aid in releasing excess energy through your body. Discontinue bad habits (you know what yours are), drink plenty of water, and try to eat heathily (avoiding alcohol and excess sugars or processed foods). This will help your body feel nourished and satisfied. You can replace any bad habits with meditation (5 to 30 minutes a day) and doing something nice for yourself, instead. Take a bath, receive a massage, get lots of extra rest, or read a book outside.

During the cleanse, student practitioners may want to give themselves a full self-healing treatment each day to help soften the internal healing that is taking place. The whole point is to start building your channel by connecting inward and upward. Taking time to be with yourself will help cultivate your awareness practice. Remember that it takes 21 days to form a habit, so this is the perfect time to be building in new patterns and behaviors that complement your healing journey.

REIKI TECHNIQUES

Throughout my years of working with clients and training countless Reiki students, I have seen many different techniques used, and I am always discovering new and intuitively guided methods that seem to result in the best benefit for the patient involved. We will be reviewing many techniques throughout the book, but let's take a look in this section at a few of the more well-known practices to get you familiar with them.

For Reiki practitioners, it's important to maintain an open channel, or connection to Source. One of the top "rules of Reiki" is to always remember that you are not the healer; you are the conduit of the energy. Therefore, you are only facilitating the treatment by allowing Source energy to move through you and make the necessary energetic adjustments to your recipient in accordance with their highest good and what their soul is ready to accept. The energy flows through a gateway that connects you to the Reiki stream, like a river of light flowing from your crown down through your hands. It's possible to feel the energy stream as a mild electric current, buzzing, warmth, or pulsing energy. This energy stream is called our "channel."

To keep your channel clear, it's always a great idea to practice one of the self-healing methods outlined in this book. This will help eliminate any blockages or stagnant energies you are holding and provide a clear pathway in which the Reiki energy can flow. When we work with the heart or crown chakra energies, the "vital charge" is a way to specifically clear any obstructions in a short amount of time. Think of this as a mini-session that provides a little shortcut to healing so your channel can remain as open as possible.

The use of symbols is another time-honored tradition in the Reiki practice. Symbols can hold different meanings for different cultures, even vastly different meanings over the course of time. It's important to carefully judge how using symbols in your practice affects your desired healing. Some practitioners find these symbols very useful and feel they contribute powerfully to their practice. We'll explore several ways to use symbols during a Reiki treatment. You can read more about symbols and what they are later in this chapter (see "Symbols," page 28).

The energy ball is a technique I used to teach in Reiki 1, but now teach in Reiki 2. Although it's an advanced technique, it's easy to learn and pick up with practice. This potent technique helps consolidate Reiki energy into a condensed, super-powered energy blast to work on more serious injuries or areas that need concentrated healing. Any wound, whether emotional or physical, will experience accelerated healing through this special practice.

Working with Reiki to remove energy cords is another great way to help your chakras function optimally. Energy cords are lines that siphon energy away from the body to another Source (this can be a person, place, or thing). They are formed between people or objects and constantly draw on our energy, causing energetic leakage. Removing these cords can be extremely helpful in coming back into wholeness and sovereignty.

Another technique often used alongside and within Reiki practices is spiritual journeying. This is a process of deep meditation to uncover subconscious patterns, traumas, core wounding, and beliefs that cause a person to become blocked, and then using other energy-clearing techniques to remove disease within the physical body, psyche, aura, or chakras.

Finally, it's possible to perform a chakra balancing using specific balancing hand positions to create equilibrium across the energy centers. This technique is especially helpful when you only have about 20 minutes to complete the healing.

Next, let's take a closer look at the hand positions and how we'll be using them during the course of this book. They are featured in each chapter and vary by chakra.

Hand Positions

A traditional Usui Reiki practice will include various hand positions developed by Dr. Hayashi early in Reiki's modern-day history. These hand positions may seem orthodox and a bit mechanical when you first start your practice, but following a protocol for placement will help eliminate the guesswork of where to focus the direction of Reiki energy. I like to teach the chakra method for this reason. By placing your hands on each chakra, you are ensuring the entire system is receiving healing. Not only is it comprehensive, it also allows you to spend time feeling the variances of each energy center and how they compare with one another. There are multiple hand positions for most chakras, as well as alternate hand positions.

As your practice progresses and you advance your skill set, you can begin to use your hands for a simple body scan to get a feel for what areas of the body are specifically calling for your attention. You may begin to intuitively swipe, blow, snap, or indicate with hand gestures around specific areas of the body. These actions help move subtle energies away from or through the body. Be sure to follow any guidance you are picking up. When resting your hands on a recipient, be respectful of their boundaries, and use only light hand placement and no actual pressure to the area, especially around vulnerable areas such as the exposed neck. For sensitive areas, you can hover the hands within the auric field to channel the energy.

Symbols

The Reiki symbols are powerful shortcuts to access energy, most of which are received in level 2. The last two, along with any advanced symbols, are passed on during mastery training (level 3). These have been handed down through the Usui lineage and were originally channeled by Dr. Usui himself. Keep in mind that universal love, not the symbols themselves, provides the energy that empowers the healing. In some Reiki lineages, symbols are not used, so get a feel for what works best for your personal practice.

> **Cho-Ku-Rei:** The **CKR** symbol is an empowerment symbol meant to accelerate or amplify healing. This is known as the *power symbol* and is received during a level 2 attunement.

> **Sei-He-Ki:** The **SHK** symbol enhances emotional release and is a symbol often chosen in times of distress or anxiety. It can be used to help release negativity or stress-induced tension (often a major key to healing), for psychic protection, and to heal addictions and codependence. This symbol is known as the emotional or mental healing symbol and is received during a level 2 attunement.

> **Ha-Sha-Ze-Sho-Nen:** The **HSZSN** symbol allows you to transcend timelines and send healing energy backward or forward in time to a recipient who is not physically present with you. It can also be used to heal the planet itself. You must select a designated time in which the healing will occur before you start the Reiki transmission, otherwise the energy will be sent to the present moment. A translation of this symbol is "No past, no present, no future." This symbol is known as the distance healing symbol and is received during a level 2 attunement.

> **Dai-Ko-Myo:** The DKM symbol is meant to harmonize energies with light. A translation of this symbol is "great shining light," and it is used as a spiritual symbol to enlighten one's path. Once you have received this symbol, traditionally you are then expected to use it in all of your healings. DKM is known as the master symbol and is received as the fourth symbol during a level 3 master attunement.

> **Raku:** The raku symbol is perhaps the most widely recognized Reiki healing symbol, and it looks like a lightning bolt. It is an alternate symbol only used at the end of an attunement to ground the practitioner. I have used this symbol at the completion of treatments if the recipient still requires

energy stabilization. This symbol may be received during level 3 or beyond, depending on the teacher.

You will see the Reiki symbols written in varied ways, likely due to modifications through different lineages as the practice has evolved. Play with them to choose the symbols you feel a personal connection to, and experiment with them during your practice.

Prepare for Healing

An essential preparation for healing is the clearing and puri-fication of our personal energy space, as well as creating the ambience necessary for peaceful and calm vibrations to flow during our Reiki sessions. This is especially important when working with multiple people, or with people in your home space. When you and your space are clear and centered, all else seems to flow easily. Your attitude affects the healing.

Dress comfortably—when you are relaxed, so is your recip-ient. You'll also want to handle any energy exchange, such as money, or any details about the session beforehand whenever possible. After smudging yourself and your space with sage, cedar, or another cleansing herb, prepare the room energetically. Make sure your recipient will be comfortable, even if you are practicing on a floor. A massage table is ideal for this practice. Beds are typically more of a challenge to navigate, so try to avoid them and opt for a recliner or pillows on a yoga mat instead, when a massage table is unavailable.

Putting on some relaxing meditative music before the treat-ment enhances the entire experience and gives your session a spa-like feel. You may choose to bring crystals into your session and place them on yourself (self-healing) or your recipient. I enjoy using one for each chakra, but there are certain special stones that may call out to be used for a healing. You may also choose to utilize essential oils in your healings. As you get more practice, your intuition will begin to inform these decisions and you will find a flow that fits your taste and abilities.

Reiki for Kids and Pets

Performing Reiki on kids and pets requires some extra attention and consideration because it can be quite different from performing Reiki on adults. Reiki is safe and gentle for the youngest children (even children in utero). It's also terrific for pets who could benefit from natural healing. But kids and pets, while both cute and cuddly, tend to move around quite a bit, making them tricky recipients. The best tip I have found over the years is to simply wait until they have gone to sleep before performing their session. If they are able to sit still for you, you may only get 10 to 15 minutes in, so there will not be time for a lot of ritual or intention beforehand. In general, both children and pets will tend to become restless or will simply get up and leave if they are done with the energy transmission. You may also be inspired to give them distance healing to provide a longer transmission, sending the energy backward or forward in time.

As with all Reiki, it's good to gain permission before starting a treatment session. If there is ever any situation in which you find yourself unable to ask for permission (this happens a lot in cases in which words are unavailable), you'll want to first obtain permission psychically. Find a quiet time to connect with the recipient's Spirit and feel into it. With kids, it's a good idea to check in with them before the treatment to gauge how they are feeling so that you can measure the success of the healing afterward.

REIKI DEGREES

There are three levels of Reiki, with the master level (level 3) taught in one or two parts. Each level trains the student to better channel the energy and introduces more advanced healing techniques. Additionally, each level requires an attunement from a Reiki Master Teacher. Let's take a closer look.

Level 1 Reiki is the basic, entry-level Reiki most common among practitioners. This is a foundational curriculum and includes hands-on healing for yourself or one other person who is physically present with you. No symbols or remote healings are involved, as all healing on this level is one-on-one. Level 1 is considered an attunement that works on a physical level, meaning that you may feel some physical side effects like fatigue, body aches, ear ringing, body temperature changes, head pressure, or other minor changes to your energy field as the energy works to clear your channel. A 21-day energy cleanse is initiated.

Level 2 Reiki is the intermediate level for practitioners looking to deepen their practice. New skills include hands-on healing for small groups, as well as distance healing (including timelines and recipients who are not physically present with you). Symbols are passed to the student at this level and advanced techniques are introduced. Generally, this is considered an attunement that works on an emotional level. You may feel heavier emotions like sadness, grief, or anxiety coming up during this time so that they can be felt and released. A second 21-day energy cleanse is initiated.

Level 3 (A) Reiki is considered the master level. I teach this in two parts, mainly because different skill sets are required at each level and not everyone will want to go on to teach or attune other practitioners. If the level 3 Reiki is taught in two parts, personal mastery and teacher training degrees are usually bestowed. Personal mastery is a foundational mastery curriculum, and in traditional Reiki schools the invitation to participate must be extended by the teacher after the student has shown commitment to spiritual growth through their ongoing practice. The practitioner receives the master level and the raku symbols, along with advanced healing techniques. This attunement works on a spiritual level. The practitioner may feel new levels of consciousness at play and a sense of lightness around them as new awareness blossoms. A third and final 21-day energy cleanse is initiated.

Level 3 (B) is also called RMT, or Reiki Master Teacher. This level trains the practitioner to pass attunements and sets them up to integrate Reiki into a professional practice. At this level, the Reiki training is complete and the practitioner is encouraged to continue practicing and passing on the gift of Reiki to their students and friends seeking healing.

Please note that Reiki mastery types are taught not only as healing modalities but also as advanced spiritual practices, to be demonstrated prior to receiving the attunement. Therefore, spiritual counseling is a large part of the journey when completing higher-level attunements. Re-attunement is suggested for those who have been away from their practice for an extended period and would like a refresher, although it is not necessary. I always take a re-attunement if my teachers offer it because it's a great opportunity to receive an energetic refresh and drop back into my practice.

REIKI FOR CHAKRA HEALING

Although Reiki and chakra work come from two very different lineages, they have really grown together to complement each other in modern-day Reiki practice. Reiki is an excellent way to heal and balance the chakras—and this book will cover everything you need to know to do just that.

As we briefly reviewed (page 18), the most widely used Reiki is a Japanese lineage called Usui Reiki. In this tradition, the hand placements follow the different areas of the body that house all the corporeal chakras. Although Reiki is being absorbed by the body during a treatment (whether hands-on or at a distance), the chakras are being treated during the energy transmission. Some practitioners like to channel above the body directly to the chakras (within the auric space) for an additional 10 minutes or so to work on chakras that feel particularly blocked.

To perform healing on multiple chakras, simply follow the hand placements in this book. A good place to start is at the crown and then work your way down to the root. Once the crown is open, it will be easier to clear the blockages because your Source connection and divine energy flow will be restored. It's also possible to spot-treat a problem chakra if you have been meditating with it and find it difficult to move the block yourself. Simply channel to the chakra you'd like to treat for 5 to 10 minutes on its own.

One way to tell if energy is blocked is by breathing deeply into the area. If you are feeling contracted, tight, or closed-off energies, or you are experiencing other telltale symptoms corresponding to that energy center, then the area is likely blocked. Work with blockages in the crown and heart first. Opening these chakras up will not only allow for greater Source energy flow, but will help you gain immediate relief. By the end of a full Reiki treatment, the chakras should be open and balanced naturally.

PART
2

REIKI HEALING

N ow that you have learned a bit about the Reiki-chakra connection, it's time to start applying what you know to help heal your chakra system. Part 2 provides an overview of each of the seven primary chakras and their main functions. Here, you'll learn how to identify when the chakras are blocked and how to work with them through Reiki to achieve balance and optimal health. We take a peek at the exciting ways you can perform your own healing treatments, as well as treatments on others. Each chapter contains highlights about the minor chakras, so you can begin to familiarize yourself with what they are and how they work with the primary chakras. Get ready to uncover this transformational Reiki-chakra connection for yourself!

CHAPTER 3

THE ROOT CHAKRA

We begin our chakra exploration with the first chakra, the root. This chapter is a basic overview of the inner workings of this vital energy center. We explore the different names the root chakra goes by, where it's located, and its associated colors and elements. This is the first primary chakra, an energy space to ground the rest of the energy centers. When this center is blocked, the rest of our energy is unable to move through and ground us. It's essential to spend time unblocking and opening this energy space through the practices reviewed here, as well as practicing lots of meditation. You'll learn what this chakra governs and its unique role within the chakra system to ground and nurture your energy.

WHAT IS THE ROOT CHAKRA?

The root chakra, or base chakra, is said to be the place where consciousness dropped into physical existence. You may also hear this referred to by the Sanskrit name *muladhara* (*mula* meaning "root" or "support," and *adhara* meaning "lower"). It's appropriate, then, as the first foundational chakra, that this energy center connects us to the earth and is most concerned with instinct and basic needs. Earth energy is very grounding, stabilizing, and strong. Think about how you feel when your body is well rested, safe to let go and relax, and overall physically comfortable. Your root space is representative of the material realm, and your physical body connects to this space. Basic survival as well as creature comforts (primal needs) are both ruled by the root. When we feel all of our primary needs are met, we can say the root space is balanced and open.

Located directly at the base of the spine and nestled into a space between your perineum and the reproductive organs, your root space is a powerful energetic center and home to sleeping kundalini energy, which lies dormant until awakened. Together, this makes the root the foundational chakra, which supports the rest of the chakra system. This energy supports the spinal column and the *kanda*, an egg-shaped energetic organ in the same location.

The element associated with your muladhara is (no surprise here) earth. Imagine red clay or rich brown soil beneath your feet as the free electrons from the ionizing earth element intermingle with your soles. The earth below you supports your every step. After all, we are children of the great mother, Mother Earth. She is the original mother, who tends to our physical needs and exchanges subtle information with us through her harmonic resonance. Just as the soil delivers nourishment to the roots of all plants and trees, the earth element delivers strength and security to our physical body. The density of this element greatly impacts the feeling of being anchored in our body vessel as our temple on Earth.

Every chakra has its own unique color band on the visible light spectrum at which it vibrates. The colors for all the chakras go in ascending order up the spine in a delightful rainbow palette. The color linked with the root space is ruby red, an intense and powerful frequency. This vibration feels primal, deep, and passionate. It's a color representing blood and love, both of which are vital to meet and sustain our basic needs. Energetically, this color also represents pure Shakti, or kundalini energy.

Taking a look at which body parts are paired with the root space, we are able to notice a foundational theme. The feet, knees, legs, lower hips, anus, and some reproductive organs are included in this chakra, along with the testes and penis (lingam) and the vagina, vaginal canal, and clitoris (the womb is part of the sacral chakra). There are certain chakras that share functionality, and the root is one of them. This chakra also governs parts of the elimination system, as well as your blood and muscular and skeletal systems. You'll find several of the chakras share certain functions, especially the lower three chakras, as so many of the body parts are closely connected and weave throughout multiple areas.

The glands that correspond to the root chakra are the adrenals. These triangular organs are located on top of your kidneys and help regulate vital bodily functions, such as hormonal balance, metabolism, the immune system, blood pressure, blood sugar levels, sleep/wake cycles, and cortisol levels. Cortisol is the body's main stress hormone; its essential functions include regulating motivation, mood, and fear.

The energy of the root chakra is very concentrated. Some of the body's heaviest and densest energies reside in the root chakra. Anger, fear, despair, loss, guilt, and shame are stored here. The root space is also responsible for a sense of safety, which normally forms early in life, along with self-esteem and identity. This chakra houses survival instincts (the fight-or-flight response) and is where we learn to self-soothe and take care of our own bodies.

Meridians, the pathways of energy that connect the chakras to the energy flow inside the body, have two main lines that flow through the root chakra—the ida and pingala lines. These represent the left (feminine) and right (masculine) sides of the body, respectively. The ida line runs down the left leg, whereas the pingala runs up the right leg.

The root space carries energies of both ecstasy as well as innocence. This fiery chakra is often associated with passion and desire. This is also where we are connected to maternal and paternal energies. Of course, it is possible to be a parent to yourself—this is a huge part of self-care. You will learn many self-care techniques for healing both of these aspects within yourself as you work with the exercises in this book. We'll discuss what this feels like for both a healthy chakra and an imbalanced chakra in the next sections (pages 42 to 46).

Treat your body with care; respect and listen to it on a regular basis to begin working with the root space more regularly. This includes taking cues from the body when you need to move, rest, or eat (how much, when, and what you eat are some points of discernment to dial into your body on a more intimate level). Not sure? Ask your body—it will tell you exactly what it needs to feel good. Your body is an amazing healer all on its own if you pay attention and take action when it's speaking to you. Now let's begin to look at some techniques to get you into your body and feel grounding through the practice of Reiki.

A Balanced Root Chakra

A balanced root chakra will be unblocked and open, allowing your grounding energy to extend from your physical body into the earth. This energy connection is vital to feeling safe and connected to your physical body, as well as to your environment. Embodiment is one of the most important human journeys we can take. One of the keys to this process is learning to trust yourself and your own capacity and strengths, and to let go of fear, doubts, and worries. Tuning in to the self promotes secure attachments between you and others, and encourages healthy boundaries (a hallmark of a balanced root chakra).

If this energy center is flourishing, your basic needs will be met, contributing to a sense of security and ease. Eventually, it will tune you into the flow of grace and prosperity. People who are very successful and have accumulated wealth on the material plane tend to have open and balanced root spaces because they have tapped into the frequency of abundance, which inherently creates more—the more you have, the more you share.

A well-balanced root chakra also promotes healthy sexuality, which for most of us has existed within the wheelhouse of toxic programming because traditional views teach that this energy is "bad" and "shameful." The healthy expression of sexual energy actually plugs you back into your divine identity by connecting you to pure streams of bliss and love. Through human connection, joining in integrity and purity (without agenda), you can enter the portal of self-discovery and eventually self-mastery. As you raise your awareness of intimacy and the person or people with whom you are sharing this energy, you will find greater self-love. In this state, higher-consciousness endeavors can be achieved, and this will aid in anchoring your vibration to the natural world as well as to those around you.

When the muladhara is healthy, presence and patience work together to create emotional stability in your auric field. When you give up the need to know and control everything, you become free to expand, grow, and evolve. This is what a balanced root chakra encourages.

The good news is that with an open and balanced root chakra, your energy in all the other main chakras is able to flow freely and feels amplified. These energies build on one another, which creates a strong and stable foundation.

An Unbalanced Root Chakra

It's relatively easy to tell when your root chakra is out of balance. If you've ever had a day in which you felt completely scattered, spacey, or destabilized (energetically or physically), you know what I mean. Since this is your center for security and primal regulation, when things are off it's usually pretty obvious. By paying close attention to your feelings, behaviors, and moods, you can start to identify how and where this is happening. It's less important to know how long the imbalance has been there or how it was created, and more important to know how to spot it so you can fix it when it crops up.

Emotionally, you may be able to feel some of your heavier emotions held within this space. It's possible to feel disconnected, insecure, fearful, or overwhelmed when there is a blockage or imbalance in this chakra. Grief and loss also tend to show up here, so if you have recently lost someone from your life, this can feel very difficult, since the sense of separation ultimately opposes our infinite, divine nature. Anger likes to show up here as well. Because we are creatures of habit, we tend to store things again and again in the same place, even after it feels resolved. That's why it's so important to regularly practice good energetic hygiene by working with energy-clearing techniques to ensure that your energy remains clean and clear.

People with root chakra imbalances also tend to have a difficult time setting boundaries because of their tendency toward self-abandonment patterns. These negative loops develop through repeated self-sabotaging behaviors, poor self-esteem development, or stuck childhood traumas. If this rings true for you, know that these can all be repaired through timeline healing work, which you can practice during the distance healing section in this chapter (page 49).

Physically, you may feel specific symptoms that indicate an imbalance in this area, including constipation, poor circulation, numbness/weakness of legs or restless legs, prostate or colon

Earth Star Chakra

The earth star chakra, also known as the zero chakra, extends below the body 6 to 12 inches underneath the feet, into the earth. This is considered a subpersonal chakra, since it exists beyond the corporeal realm. The earth star is like an anchor, tethering you to earth consciousness. It includes a grounding element, much like the root chakra, and this chakra feels galactic and ancient all at once. Perhaps it is because the earth contains all the records of our DNA, ancestry, and human history.

By learning about your earth star chakra, you can tap into ancient knowledge held within your akashic records, which contain the database of your past, present, and future timelines on earth and beyond. The earth star chakra can help you connect to collective as well as individual timelines to access the highest possible outcomes in any current situation, while helping heal and soften any past traumas (many of which are held and passed down through ancestors).

Another important function of this subpersonal energy center is to help stabilize your entire energy system. As your energy opens up with Reiki, and continues to expand during this time of awakening, your spinal channel will need a deeper way to stay balanced and rooted. As far as your light energy extends upward to Source, it must also extend downward into our Mother Earth. Your earth star serves a very important function by creating balance within your chakra system, grounding your entire chakra system and allowing it to grow and expand.

issues, and general sluggishness or adrenal fatigue. You may experience lower back or knee problems, or pelvic issues such as pain and inflammation. Since the elimination organs share some functions with the root space, bladder and kidney issues can also indicate root chakra blockages, although they are more commonly found within the sacral chakra.

Imbalances in this energy center may present as behavioral issues, such as eating disorders, unnecessary spending, gambling problems, or other compulsive/addictive behaviors that don't seem rational. This is because when the center for security is compromised, we tend to overcompensate for what we are lacking by attempting to fill it with other activities. This usually ends up just masking the problem if the energy behind the issue isn't addressed. Luckily, this can be helped through Reiki healing.

HEALING THE ROOT CHAKRA

This section introduces two Reiki healing applications for the root chakra: one for healing yourself and others, and one for distance healing. This technique builds on skills needed to get to know your energy channel, understand how Reiki works, and explore what feels good or appropriate for the level of healing and effects desired. As you are practicing, play with what feels good, and open a dialogue when you are sharing the energy with another person so they can provide feedback, which will be a valuable tool as you grow your Reiki practice.

These techniques include working with the Reiki symbols, which you may or may not be accustomed to using, depending on the Reiki level to which you are attuned. There are several ways to work with the various symbols in each exercise, but because you don't need the symbols to practice Reiki, feel free to leave them out. The following section reviews how to use Reiki for self-healing, healing of others, and distance healing, and it provides alternate hand position holds.

Specifically, I cover the CKR symbol (see "Symbols," chapter 2, page 28). You'll learn how to use it in conjunction with complementary hand positions to open and unblock the root chakra. CKR is the power symbol, meant to restore vitality and strength, and to facilitate powerful clearing. Additionally, you can practice with the root space at a distance, incorporating a technique to deliver healing while grounding the individual using the raku symbol.

Healing the Self and Others

This practice explains basic hand positions for working on yourself, as well as an alternate way to work with Reiki by incorporating the CKR symbol. Allow plenty of time during the treatment so it feels spacious. The suggested time limit for the root chakra is 10 to 15 minutes, since it is a large energy center that covers multiple areas of the body. Come to a centered place beforehand through gassho or meditation so you are at your best to deliver the healing. Set an intention that the healing will work toward the greatest benefit within the most beneficial timeline. This will ensure all healing is delivered exactly where it is needed and works appropriately for the highest good.

When performing this treatment on someone else, the hand positions remain the same. Due to the sensitive nature of this area of the body, however, it's important to gauge the comfort level of the recipient and limit the use of the hands-on healing to the knees and below. When you are working on any sensitive or private area, keep your hands in the auric field within a foot's distance around the body to ensure the comfort and safety of both you and the recipient.

Follow these steps for this posture for self-healing:

1. Place the hands on the body, below the abdomen, on either side of the pelvis bones. Your palms may gently rest on your body, or they can hover above this region if that is more comfortable.

2. Practice using the CKR symbol here by drawing the symbol with your finger(s) over the pelvis. If you are feeling inspired, push the symbol into your root space gently, swiping down from the aura toward the body. Remember that we use this symbol to amplify the energy. Try it to see if this makes a difference in how you feel during your treatment.

3. Smile, relax, and intend to channel Reiki energy to this area for three to five minutes, or as long as you are intuitively guided to do so.

4. Your eyes may be open or closed and your attention should be as it is during meditation—a soft focus on a gentle, loving awareness stream as you channel.

5. Next, move your hands to both knees. Continue to channel Reiki for three to five minutes here, or until guided to move on.

6. When you feel ready, guide your hands to your ankles as best as you can and continue to channel for three to five minutes.

   Note: In Reiki, I always suggest not blocking the flow of energy streaming from the soles of the feet, as there is a great amount of energy being released, and it flows in descending waves down and out of the body through the feet.

7. When you are finished, come back into gassho to signal the end of the treatment. Share a moment of gratitude with your guides and Source energy for any assistance received.

Distance Healing

When performing distance healing, there are a few rules to keep in mind prior to starting your treatment. Always use the HSZSN symbol if you have received it in attunement. You must also always pick a time and place (when and where) the recipient will be receiving the healing. This is imperative, as the healing will be sent immediately in real time if this part is not specified. Since the Reiki is a quantum energy, the beautiful thing about it is that it can be sent to different timelines to effectively soften or dissolve old timelines and stories, freeing any trapped energy along the way.

Follow these steps for distance healing:

1. Draw the HSZSN symbol with your finger(s) directly into the space in front of you to open up the session. You may say it out loud or have it written down nearby, along with the name of the person receiving the healing as well as the time and place they will receive it.

If you are sending Reiki energy to yourself, you can send the energy backward or forward in time to an event or situation that needs healing. Make sure you include this in your intention when drawing the HSZSN symbol.

2. Imagine that you are there with your recipient. Hold them in your mind intentionally and focus on opening your Reiki channel as you relax and breathe.

3. Repeat the steps from the first exercise, moving down the pelvis, knees, and ankles.

4. Complete the session by drawing the raku symbol to help ground the recipient. This symbol should be used to provide extra stabilizing energy, but only at the end of the session.

   Bonus: Practice distance healing on yourself while holding the intention to heal a past timeline by sending energy to yourself around an event in which you experienced trauma, sadness, grief, or loss. There's no need to relive all the pain, but open yourself up to the healing available through delivering Reiki to that specific moment. Do this for 5 to 10 minutes until you feel a shift or softening.

5. Come back to gassho to signal completion and give thanks.

Mantras and Affirmations

A mantra is a repeated syllable or sound that helps with concentration during meditation. Since we are working with the chakras, it's possible to incorporate a mantra into your self-healing techniques if you need help focusing your mind. Regular meditation will make focusing easier over time. If your mind naturally wanders, just draw your attention back to your breath or mantra. Verbal mantras are best used in both self and distance Reiki but should not be used during healing someone else because doing so would disrupt the experience for the recipient.

The mantra for the root space is "LAM." Chanting this mantra, silently or aloud, helps stabilize your energy and instill a feeling of security by infusing the earth element into the root chakra. Let this syllable reverberate throughout your lower body. By chanting "LAM," you will empower connection with your physical body. This can help you feel safe and grounded during a session.

Affirmations are supportive statements that encourage positivity while helping you align yourself through intention. The affirmation seed for your root chakra is "I am." You can pair this seed statement with words to help connect you to your root.

Here are some examples:

→   I am safe and secure.

→   I am grounded and stable.

→   I am trusting myself.

→   I am whole and complete.

→   I am abundant in all ways.

Try incorporating some or all of these affirmations during practice or when you are ending a session. Remember, there is no wrong way to do this, so have fun with it!

CHAPTER 4

THE SACRAL CHAKRA

Moving up the spinal column from the root chakra, we come to your second or sacral chakra—home of your deep emotions and self-expression. This chapter provides a basic overview of the inner workings of this deep and watery energy center. Sacral energies are often misunderstood, as so much distortion exists around sensuality, sexuality, and self-love. It's time to bring back understanding around human connection, the natural polarity of the feminine and masculine archetypes, and the balance between the internal landscape of intimacy and the outward expression of the sacral energies. With a focus on the emotional and physical links this chakra has with the body, you'll learn more about this vital energy center.

WHAT IS THE SACRAL CHAKRA?

The sacral chakra is the next energy center up the spinal channel. This is where you access how to give, receive, and respond, as it's the feeling center of your chakra system. Coincidentally, it's located in your lower gut, which houses your microbiome (some scientists believe the microbiome has a direct effect on your personality and expression). Another name for the sacral chakra is the Sanskrit term *svadhisthana* (*sva* meaning "self" and *histhana* meaning "established"). The name draws on the principles of self-care, resilience, and inner authority. This energy center connects us to our own creative expression and sensuality and is concerned with interpersonal connections with others. The sacral space is representative of the unseen realm of emotions, responses, creativity, and balance. When emotions are well adjusted and we feel our expression is not only allowed, but welcome, our sacral chakra will thrive.

Located just up from the root space, the sacral chakra is about two inches below the navel at the abdomen. Nestled between your tailbone and sacrum (the triangular area at the small of your back), the sacral space is a sacred vortex of creation located between the navel and internal sex organs. The sacral chakra shares certain functions and systems with the root and solar plexus chakras. These are all interrelated and holistically connected, so some of the energies blend between these fluid-like energy centers. For example, both the root and the sacral chakras address masculine and feminine essence as well as issues with sensuality and sexuality.

The element associated with the svadhisthana is water. Visualize turquoise ocean waves lapping at your feet, or a cool, babbling mountain stream running over rocks. Water energy is cleansing, soothing, and hydrating to the soul. It helps wash away impurities, providing a good "reset." Water teaches us how to go with the flow and detach from expectations and outcomes with grace. This element connects you to your sensitivities, depth, and inner artist. It delivers compassionate care and perspective exactly when you are in need of it. The water element here is denser than fire (solar plexus) and less dense than earth (root chakra), representing fluidity and cohesion.

The color associated with the sacral space is vibrant orange, a bright and joyful frequency. This vibration combines the intensity of red with the exuberance of yellow. It's a color representing warmth, creativity, enthusiasm, success, determination, and adventure, and it energetically resonates with the vibration of excitement.

Taking a look at which body parts are paired with the sacral space, we find many major organs with primary body functions exist here (and some that overlap among chakras). The hips, kidneys, bladder, large intestines, lower back, and some internal reproductive organs are included in this chakra. The kidneys and bladder are also part of the body's elimination system, and because they become engorged with water (and need this element to function), they are also included in the sacral region.

Of course, there is some variance between the sexes on what exactly is covered by this chakra. For males, the testes are included (with the lingam) in the root chakra. For females, the cervix and uterus are considered to be part of the sacral chakra. There are certain chakras that share functions, and the sacral chakra is one of them. For example, the sacral and root chakras both govern the pelvis and lower vertebrae.

The glands that correspond to the sacral chakra are the gonads or internal sex organs. For females, this includes the ovaries, and for males, the testicles. These serve a major purpose in the reproductive system. Females have two ovaries, which release ova (eggs) on a monthly basis, indicating potential fertility. They are home to hormones like estrogen and progesterone. During ovulation, the ovaries release one egg (or sometimes more) per menstrual cycle. In males, the testes are responsible for housing the sperm, the male reproductive cells. Together, these glands form the sacral creation station, responsible for regenerative life as we know it.

The energy of the sacral chakra plugs us into our sense of intimacy and belonging. The closeness we feel with other human beings, how we exchange subtle energy, and how we experience pleasure all operate within this space. Our ability to perceive and feel impacts our connection with our inner world as well as how we operate in the outer world. Just as water can hold great depth, the energies here also hold great depth. Unexpressed and expressed emotions live here, and they can affect how we treat others and, therefore, how we are treated. There's a saying, "You must feel it to heal it," and that is exactly the case when you are working with trapped emotions. Energetic imprints from past lovers are also stored here, so a Reiki womb cleansing is vital to keeping this chakra autonomous and clear.

The two main meridian lines, the ida and pingala, begin in the navel center (see "The Hara Line," page 59), flow down into the root chakra, and then down or up each leg. As a reminder, these represent both the left (feminine) and right (masculine) sides of the body. The ida line runs down the left leg, whereas the pingala runs up the right leg. The following section addresses more about how these energies work together and what it means to achieve balance here.

A Balanced Sacral Chakra

A primary hallmark of a balanced sacral chakra is the ability to establish deeper relationships in the world. The sacral chakra feels supported enough to do this once the root space is firmly established, we feel totally present in our bodies, and our physical needs are met. With an open sacral chakra, you are motivated to engage with others socially and intimately, which is necessary to form long-lasting bonds and all other types of relationships. An open sacral chakra also means being able to check in with yourself and read your emotional needs well.

An open sacral chakra is also associated with accessing one's creativity. When your artistic side is stimulated, projects and art are allowed to flow. You may feel tuned in to new passions like writing, painting, music, or dance, and will start to notice that your self-expression and the way you show up in the world play a part in creating your entire reality.

Another indicator of a healthy sacral chakra is the balance of energies that are harmonizing within this space. The feminine (lunar) and masculine (solar) energies exist here, and oftentimes we lean into one or the other. These don't refer to sex or gender, but to the universal energies of yin and yang. The feminine energies govern deep connectivity, letting go, receptivity, and flow, while the masculine energies are all about taking charge, productivity, achievement, measurable outcomes, and resolutions. By achieving harmony, these energies of polarity are free to dance and play to their natural, balanced rhythms.

While the root chakra is thought to be linked to sexuality and passion, the sacral chakra shares some of these inherent functions but focuses more on the expression of sensuality, pleasure, needs, and desires. This watery chakra is responsible for sex drive or libido, as arousal is a natural physical response linked with the innate function of hormonal release. Libido operates on a spectrum, and there is no such thing as a universal "normal." Try not to judge yourself if you aren't feeling connected to feelings of desire—many factors influence and are involved in libido. If you are in touch with your desires and needs, this is a good indicator your sacral chakra is open.

If it's your goal to get back in touch with this side of yourself, you may want to perform some Reiki healing so you can reestablish the connection to your deep, inner well of emotions. The next section provides more techniques to get your emotional energies back into balance through the practice of Reiki.

An Unbalanced Sacral Chakra

When your sacral chakra is underperforming, accessing your emotions at all can be difficult, especially if you have gone through trauma, whether in childhood or more recently. When emotions are suppressed, you might feel numb. This sort of detachment is a way the ego protects itself from experiencing unpleasant feelings like anger, sadness, anxiety, or stress. If you are avoiding people, places, or activities, creating or maintaining relationships may be difficult. Plugging back into your emotional self takes effort, which is one of the top benefits of using Reiki energy.

Low or blocked sacral energy can contribute to depression, manic or emotional instability, loss of imagination or creativity, and addiction. If you are at a dead end, experiencing resistance to doing the things you once loved, unable to finish projects, or have lost excitement in your life where you once felt motivation, you might be suffering from a sacral imbalance. When you are feeling depressed, it's hard to be present in your body or to stay inspired. Inspiration has to come from within—as with all things, you vibrationally have to be a match for it in order for it to show up in your life. Creativity holds a high frequency of growth and expansion, and it will flow easily to you when your sacral energies are clear.

Sexual dysfunction is another indication that imbalances exist in this chakra. Problems can occur during any phase of the sexual response cycle, preventing you from experiencing satisfying sex. You may experience problems with desire or climax, or, pain during sex. In general, these issues stem from a core wound—the lack of intimate bonds with others from an early age. This lack of intimate childhood bonds can show up as reproductive issues or hormonal imbalances in both men and women. They can also create insecurities stemming from poor self-esteem and confidence.

Finally, difficulty showing love or affection may be another sign of a sacral imbalance. The withholding might be voluntary

The Hara Line

The hara line is a small, minor chakra, sometimes called the *dantian*, located about two inches below the *hara* or "navel" within the sacral chakra. Although certain Eastern systems record the hara line as an off-body chakra located in the auric field, we will be looking at it in terms of its corporeal nature. This small but powerful energy point on the body is well-known in Chinese medicine and plays an important role within the meridian system. This point is called the "sea of chi (ki)" and is responsible for splitting three energy lines, or meridians: one down each of the legs and one into the earth (where it meets the earth star chakra). This minor chakra is a potent meeting place of both corporeal and auric energies and is used as a focal point in traditional energy medicine, as well as Reiki, to circulate vital creative energies and bring ki (energy) into the body.

The microcosmic orbit is a breathwork technique that directs the breath and cultivates more ki within the chakra system. This technique is used in Reiki Master Teacher training in order to pass attunements and can be worked with to help energize and revitalize ourselves when feeling fatigued or low in energy. You won't need to know how to use this at the beginner level, but you can practice breathing into the hara line to intentionally increase energy any time you want to try it out.

and proactive but, in many cases, this pattern is the result of trauma, neglect, or abuse. It could indicate a lack of development in childhood or adolescence during which your empathy was inhibited. You may also struggle with accepting other people's emotions—especially if your emotions weren't accepted when you were young. Although all of these responses may have served you at one point in time, as adults we repeat behavioral responses and continue to use them even when they no longer serve us. Re-patterning and restructuring are possible, especially when there is a strong commitment to change.

HEALING THE SACRAL CHAKRA

This section introduces two Reiki healing applications for the sacral chakra: one for healing yourself and others, and one for distance healing. These techniques build on skills needed to get to know your own energy channel, understand how Reiki works, and explore what feels good or appropriate for the level of healing and effects desired. As you are practicing, play with what feels good, and open a dialogue when you are sharing the energy with another person so they can provide valuable feedback.

These techniques include working with the Reiki symbols, which you may or may not be accustomed to using, depending on the Reiki level to which you are attuned. There are several ways to work with the various symbols in each exercise, but because you don't need the symbols to practice Reiki, feel free to leave them out. The following section reviews how to use Reiki for self-healing, healing of others, and distance healing.

I cover how to use the SHK symbol to form an energy ball, specifically for healing emotional distress (see "Symbols," chapter 2, page 28). SHK is the emotional healing symbol meant to calm, soothe, and restore peace to the subtle body. Additionally, I provide corresponding hand positions to open and unblock the sacral chakra and explain how to work on a distance healing technique using the energy ball in a new way.

Healing the Self and Others

In this exercise, you'll learn the basic hand positions for working on your sacral chakra, as well as an alternate way to work with the Reiki by forming an energy ball. We'll also incorporate the powerful SHK symbol, which is used for emotional healing. Allow plenty of time during the treatment so it feels spacious. The suggested time limit for the sacral chakra is 10 to 15 minutes, since it is a lower energy center with several hand positions. Come to a centered place beforehand through gassho or meditation so you are at your best to deliver the healing. Set an intention that the healing will work for the greatest benefit within the most beneficial timeline. This will ensure all healing is delivered exactly where needed and works appropriately for the highest good.

Follow these steps for this posture for self-healing:

1. Practice using the SHK symbol here by drawing the symbol with your finger(s) over the palm to open up the session.

2. Begin to form an energy ball by making a small "shelf" and "wall" with both hands: one flat, upward-facing palm connecting with the edge of your other hand, which is sitting at 90 degrees.

3. Allow Reiki energy to descend into the open palm for a minute or so, then gently sculpt the energy with your other hand, patting it into the shape of an energy ball.

4. Slide the bottom "shelf" hand up to your sacral chakra and slowly push the energy ball into your body with your free hand. Allow it to be absorbed.

5. Use traditional hand placements for the remainder of the treatment.

6. Place the hands flat on the body, on the abdomen below the navel and above the pelvis and hip bones. Your palms may gently rest on your body, or they can hover above this region if more comfortable.

7. Smile, relax, and intend to channel Reiki energy to this area for three to five minutes, or as long as you are intuitively guided to do so.

8. Repeat channeling to the hips for three to five minutes.

9. Move your hands to the lower back and repeat channeling for three to five minutes. (This step is only for self-healing.) Your eyes may be open or closed and your attention should be as it is during meditation: a soft focus on a gentle, loving awareness stream as you channel.

10. When you are finished, either move on to another chakra for more healing or come back into gassho to signal the end of the treatment. Share a moment of gratitude with your guides and Source energy for any assistance received.

Keep in mind that there is no need to flip someone over when performing a Reiki treatment, as the energy flows where it's needed. Unless specifically requested, the energy is just fine being channeled to the body as it faces upward.

Distance Healing

When performing distance healing, there are a few rules to keep in mind prior to starting your treatment. As mentioned in chapter 3 (page 49), always use the HSZSN symbol if you have received it in attunement. You must always pick a time and place (when and where) the recipient will be receiving the healing. This is imperative, because otherwise the healing will be sent immediately in real time.

Follow these steps for distance healing:

1. Draw the HSZSN symbol with your finger(s) directly into the space in front of you to open up the session. You may say aloud the name of the person receiving the healing (or have it written down nearby) as well as the time and place they will receive it.

    If you are sending Reiki energy to yourself, you can send the energy backward or forward in time to an event or situation that needs healing. Make sure you include this in your intention when drawing the HSZSN symbol.

2. Draw the SHK symbol for emotional healing in your palm, and then form an energy ball around it, as in the previous exercise (page 61).

3. Imagine the room your recipient is in. Hold them in your mind intentionally and focus on opening your Reiki channel as you relax and breathe.

4. Visualize the energy ball in the room with your recipient. Play with pushing it into their field, into a body part or

location around the sacral chakra, or expanding the ball out to 12 feet, filling the room they are in.

5. Repeat the steps from the first exercise, moving your hands to the abdomen and hips to perform the treatment.

   Bonus: Practice distance healing on yourself while holding the intention to heal a past timeline by sending energy to yourself around an event in which you experienced trauma, sadness, grief, or loss. There's no need to relive all the pain, but open yourself up to the healing available through delivering Reiki to that specific moment. Do this for 5 to 10 minutes until you feel a shift or softening.

6. Come back to gassho to signal completion and give thanks.

Mantras and Affirmations

As mentioned in the last chapter (page 51), a mantra is a repeated syllable or sound that helps in concentration during meditation. The mantra for the sacral space is "VAM." Chanting this mantra, silently or aloud, helps restore balance and creativity and wash away old emotions by infusing the water element into the sacral chakra. Let this syllable reverberate throughout your lower body. By chanting "VAM," you will empower your Shakti or energy flow and sacral energies to awaken. The affirmation seed for your sacral chakra is "I feel."

Here are some examples:

→   I feel that I belong.

→   I feel balanced and energized.

→   I have permission to feel all of my deep emotions.

→   I embrace pleasure.

→   My sexuality is sacred.

→   I allow creative energy to flow through me into all I do.

CHAPTER 5

THE SOLAR PLEXUS CHAKRA

Your solar plexus chakra, situated in your core, is a power-house of vital energy. This is your third chakra and the first of the lower physical chakras. The home of your confidence and willpower, this is your body's battery. When a battery is low, all other functions, especially vital power, will be affected. This chapter provides a basic overview of the inner workings of this bright and fiery energy center and suggests ways to keep it operating at its peak through Reiki. We explore the emotional and physical influences this energy center plays in your health and well-being, and you will gain an understanding of the unique role it plays within the chakra system to sustain vital energies.

WHAT IS THE SOLAR PLEXUS CHAKRA?

Just under the curve of your rib cage, in the upper belly, is your third chakra, the solar plexus. The name draws influence from the sun in our solar system, the radiant centerpiece that powers all of life. Like the sun, this energy center is a huge vortex and one of the most active in the body. You can always tangibly feel waves of energy moving when performing Reiki around this area, which tells us that this center is a quite lively and strong chakra; it is all about purpose, authority, and inner strength. Feelings of willpower and self-control are also centered here. This chakra governs restraint and motivation, helping you quit while you're ahead or keep going to the finish line.

I have helped many clients over the years attain manifestation goals, all through chakra work, and especially by using the solar plexus. Since this space is considered your source of drive, ambition is born here. An idea generated in this space is just waiting for inspired action to be born. This luminous portal puts a fire underneath you to accelerate your desires. When you feel excited, you're tuning in to a gut feeling first. This area is also sometimes referred to as the lower third eye because it's the first response mechanism we have to really feel our deeper instinctual self.

Another name for the solar plexus is *manipura* (Sanskrit for "city of jewels" or "lustrous gem"). The name in its loose translation draws on the principle of the brightness or fire of this chakra and its ability to create change. A place of inner transformation, this energy center connects us to our inner resilience and dedication, and it is most concerned with our sense of self. Our solar plexus is representative of our inner landscape and personal identity—a composite of personality traits, including beliefs, aspirations, and values. It develops over the course of our life, evolving based on the choices we make and the directions we choose to go. This ultimately impacts self-esteem and ambitions or goals.

Located at the diaphragm in the upper abdomen, the solar plexus is not only an energy nexus in the center of the body but also a nerve cluster that exists within the belly (also called the celiac plexus, a complex bundle of nerves and ganglia that sits in front of the stomach). This location contains some of the densest and most important energies of the body. The solar plexus shares certain functions and systems with other energy centers, which are interrelated and holistically connected. Some of the energies overlap. Both the solar plexus and the sacral chakras, for example, address various parts of the digestive system, while parts of the kidneys and adrenals are also jointly managed by the root and solar plexus chakras.

The element associated with the manipura is fire. Fire energy is intense, alive, ferocious, transformative, and sometimes downright dangerous. Its ability to burn is always present, so working with it requires measured doses. Since this element is all about the energy it creates, tuning in to this personal power creates ripples of energy that emanate from your being. Fire must also be vigilant to not use up all its resources and burn itself out. When you are feeling that your energy has been expended, resting and recharging may be on the menu for getting this chakra back into full gear. Fire teaches us that transformation is always possible and that you have the power within you to change if you so desire. The fire element here is denser than air (heart) and less dense than water (sacral).

The color linked with the solar plexus is bright yellow, a sunny and exuberant frequency. This vibration is a pure primary color. It's a color of excitement, enthusiasm, success, and optimism, resonating with the vibration of charisma and confidence.

Taking a look at which body parts are paired with the solar plexus, we find that many major organs with primary body functions exist here (and some that overlap with other chakras). The rest of the digestive organs, which support corresponding physical processes, are included in this chakra. Consider the fire power needed to turn food into nutrients, and nutrients into energy—to *burn* calories. The parts managed by the solar plexus are the stomach, gallbladder, pancreas, liver, spleen, lower esophagus, and small intestines. Skin and breath are also included in this chakra, as are the muscles of the belly and mid-back.

The glands that correspond to the solar plexus are the endocrine and exocrine glands of the pancreas. This organ sits under the stomach against the small intestine, and its primary function is to release hormones like insulin, which regulates the amount of glucose in the blood, and enzymes which help digest proteins. The adrenal cortex—responsible for balancing sex hormones, salt in the blood, and cortisol (which manages stress)—is also managed here. The critical functions for regulating the fight-or-flight response and keeping the organs running smoothly make this chakra essential to the body's central nervous system.

A Balanced Solar Plexus

The ability to rely on oneself is a major contributor to self-esteem, especially early in life. This ability helps confidence grow as we lean into self-trust and develop character and determination—all traits of someone whose solar plexus has been well developed. A person with an open and balanced solar plexus will be comfortable in their identity and exude an inner authority. Inner authority is the body's innate intelligence—the ability to be comfortable and secure in your decision-making. Every day we are faced with endless decisions, from big to small, and all of them take energy, along with proper discernment, to make the best choices. With an open solar plexus, these decisions will come easily and you'll learn to trust your decision-making skills.

Just as the sun perpetually shines, so does the inner fire that lights our path. Like the sun, we are constantly drawing from our inner resources, which must be established over time. Self-reliance sets the tone for a high vibrational solar plexus as we grow in dependability and responsibility.

A balanced solar plexus fosters the ability to sustain energy levels, balance assertiveness, and facilitate cooperation and ease within our relationships. Another elevated function of a balanced solar plexus is productivity. Being able to regulate energy levels and focus is key to efficiency. This is especially valuable if you are a leader or self-starter, or if you have an entrepreneurial mind. People who are naturally inclined toward these tendencies flow with the frequency of abundance and tend to obtain powerful occupations and material wealth in the world. Healing this chakra can restore momentum on your path and propel you forward in life. You will feel in control of the direction your life and will have the energy to bring yourself to where you want to be.

The solar plexus governs much of the digestive system, so it is associated with smooth digestion and a healthy metabolic rate. People with opened and balanced solar plexus chakras rarely get stomach ulcers, indigestion, or irritable bowel syndrome (IBS). They also have less anxiety, which is stored in this energy center. Most of the energy moves through, transmuted by the body, when this center is open. Powerful solar plexus energy pulses and flows through us—it is the light of the sun burning away all that does not serve us.

When this energy is flowing freely, you'll also have a much easier time manifesting and attracting people, places, and things in your life, picking up on synchronicities around you more frequently and providing confirmation that you are on the right path. Animal totems, numbers, and repeated symbols or words can also start showing up to point you in the right direction—pay attention to what you think they mean.

An Unbalanced Solar Plexus

An underperforming or out-of-balance solar plexus may produce intensity, both emotionally and physically. Because this chakra is so active, it's easy to notice when something is off. Physical symptoms—including such digestion-related issues as food intolerance, bloating, gas, heartburn, gallstones, IBS, or ulcers—may appear after prolonged blockages. Low or blocked solar plexus energy can also show up as emotional imbalances. Blocked energies in this chakra contribute to anxiety, irritability, or loss of creativity. You may not be motivated to wake up and perform

The Trust Bridge

The space between your solar plexus and heart chakras is a sacred space called the *trust bridge*. It's a minor chakra point and therefore serves as a smaller vortex of energy connecting the two energy centers, located right above the bottom of the rib cage and sternum. In this overlap, there are many shared energies. The heart chakra, which you'll learn more about in the next chapter (page 81), is the first of the upper spiritual chakras, connecting the etheric energies of the astral planes to the physical planes of human existence (so it is a special portal all on its own). And, as you have learned, the solar plexus is the first of the lower physical chakras. So the bridge lies right in the valley between the two hemispheres of physical and spiritual. It's this place that holds your gut instinct and "lower third eye."

When we think of the concept of trust, we know that inherent trust in others inhabits the root chakra, along with all our basic needs. However, as we progress through life, we'll need to sharpen our discernment and trust in our own abilities to gauge situations, choose the right partnerships, and rely on our heart-led consciousness to lead us in the proper direction. There is no second-guessing when this chakra is used appropriately. After our heart feels a vibration, our trust bridge essentially checks in, allowing us to feel more deeply into our yes or no. This is your gut reaction—trust it as you would your third eye intuition.

your normal routine, or you may feel uninspired to finish projects you started. Though everyone experiences one or more of these periods at times, they are less likely to happen when the chakras are clear and open. Waves of inspiration come and go, but when you get yourself into a rut, thinking or imagining a life beyond what you're currently experiencing can be a challenge. It can take a lot of mental energy to turn the ship around.

More indications of an imbalanced solar plexus may include feeling impulsive or having unexplained cravings, insomnia, abdominal cramping or tightness, high blood pressure, or stomach aches. Since your metabolism is regulated in the liver, weight gain or loss and your body's ability to convert food into energy can be affected if your solar plexus is blocked. You may also struggle with dysfunction in your body's natural stress-response system. Elevated cortisol translates to feelings of stress since your center for the fight-or-flight response is located here as well. The sympathetic nervous system regulates this trigger response in the body, which provides the body with a burst of energy to respond to perceived dangers in the environment. This is an automatic physiological reaction to events interpreted as elevated threats, and the body can have trouble deescalating when it experiences a prolonged stress response. Long-term activation of the stress response can create an overproduction of cortisol and be disruptive to almost all body processes.

Finally, struggles with confidence or with feeling disconnected from one's purpose are signs of low energy in the manipura. Self-assurance comes from the appreciation of your innate abilities, gifts, and talents. It's easy to let the inner critic steal the show, but it's important to remember that you can consciously work with insecurities and limiting beliefs to curb the effect they have on your confidence and quality of life. The more you quietly believe in yourself, the more you will attract others on the same positive wavelength. This will allow you to explore a purposeful path, reconnecting yourself to those things that light you up and make you excited to be alive.

HEALING THE SOLAR PLEXUS

This section introduces two Reiki healing applications for the solar plexus: one for healing yourself and others, and one for distance healing. This technique builds on skills needed to get to know your energy channel, understand how Reiki works, and explore what feels good or appropriate for the level of healing and effects desired. As you are practicing, play with what feels good, and open a dialogue when you are sharing the energy with another person so they can provide valuable feedback.

These techniques include working with the Reiki symbols, which you may or may not be accustomed to using, depending on the Reiki level to which you are attuned. There are several ways to work with the various symbols in each exercise, but because you don't need the symbols to practice Reiki, feel free to leave them out. The following section reviews how to use Reiki for self-healing, healing of others, and distance healing.

For both self-healing and distance healing, I cover how to use the CKR symbol with traditional hand placements (see "Symbols," chapter 2, page 28). CKR is the physical healing symbol meant to amplify healing energy in the body.

If you don't use the symbols, that's okay, too! See what feels best for your practice.

Healing the Self and Others

This section provides the basic hand positions for working on your solar plexus chakra and offers suggestions for alternate ways to work with Reiki for cord cutting. There are also more opportunities for practice with the powerful CKR symbol, used for amplifying and accelerating healing. Allow plenty of time for the treatment so that it feels spacious. The suggested time limit for the solar plexus chakra is 10 to 15 minutes. Come to a centered place within beforehand through gassho or meditation so you are at your best to deliver the healing, and set an intention that the healing will work for the greatest benefit within the most beneficial timeline. This will ensure all healing is delivered exactly where needed and works appropriately for the highest good.

Follow these steps for this posture for self-healing:

1. Practice using the CKR symbol by drawing the symbol with your finger(s) over the solar plexus or within the aura of the recipient.

2. Perform traditional hand placements. First, place the hands on the belly, below the rib cage and above the navel. Both hands should be in line with each other all the way across the belly and flat against the body.

3. Smile, relax, and intend to channel Reiki energy to this area for three to five minutes or as long as you are intuitively guided to do so.

4. Move both hands to either side of the belly and to the side of the body. Repeat channeling to the hips for three to five minutes.

   Alternate hand position: Practice doing one side at a time. For example, place both hands on the right side of the body, then both hands on the left side of the body. Repeat channeling for three minutes per side.

5. Move both hands to the middle back. Repeat channeling for three minutes. (This step is only for self-healing.)

6. With your eyes closed in meditation as you are channeling, ask your guides if there are any unhealthy energetic cords present that are no longer serving your highest good. You will either sense these intuitively or be able to "see" them with your inner vision. Go with your instinct on where you feel they are. These may be in the solar plexus, but they may also connect to other chakras.

7. Reach into the aura and snip the cords with your fingers, as though you were practicing a cutting motion. Snip until the cords are severed. Then, place your hands on the area(s) the cords came from and invite healing. Allow the other ends of the cords to go back to whomever or wherever they originated from, peacefully.

8. When you are finished, either move on to another chakra for more healing or come back into gassho to signal the end of the treatment. Share a moment of gratitude with your guides and Source energy for any assistance received.

Keep in mind that there is no need to flip someone over when performing a Reiki treatment, as the energy flows where it's needed. Unless specifically requested, the energy is just fine being channeled to the body as it faces upward.

Distance Healing

Make sure to use your HSZSN symbol if you have received it in attunement, specifying a time and place your recipient will be receiving the healing. Proceed to the next steps when you are ready.

Follow these steps for distance healing:

1. Draw the HSZSN symbol with your finger(s) directly into the space in front of you to open up the session. You may say the name of the person receiving the healing aloud (or have it written down nearby) as well as the time and place they will receive it.

   If you are sending Reiki energy to yourself, you can send the energy backward or forward in time to an event or situation that needs healing. Make sure you include this in your intention when drawing the HSZSN symbol.

2. Repeat the steps from the previous exercise; visualize the person there with you, and move your hands to the belly and side of the body to perform the treatment.

3. Visualize the CKR symbol for amplified healing in light letters or pictures. With your intention, move this symbol into the belly of the recipient and imagine it being absorbed. Repeat a few times if desired.

   Bonus: Practice distance healing on yourself while holding the intention to heal a past timeline by sending energy to yourself around an event in which you experienced disconnection or trauma. Do this for 5 to 10 minutes until you feel a shift or softening. You might practice with the SHK symbol as well to see if this makes a difference for you.

4. Come back to gassho to signal completion and give thanks.

Mantras and Affirmations

The mantra for the solar plexus space is "RAM." Chanting this mantra, either silently or aloud, helps build energy and motivation by infusing the fire element into the solar plexus chakra. Let this syllable reverberate throughout your belly, back, and lower body. By chanting "RAM," you will empower your connection to your life's purpose. The affirmation seed for your solar plexus is "I do."

Here are some examples:

→   I am in alignment with the abundant flow of the Universe.

→   I am strong, brave, and capable.

→   I do honor myself.

→   I do choose the best for myself.

→   I do celebrate my unique purpose on this planet.

CHAPTER 6

~~~

THE HEART CHAKRA

This sacred space of the heart is one of embodied love. What could be a greater earth lesson than learning how to be in harmony on this planet of emotions? It all starts from within the heart. This is where we learn self-love, compassion for others, empathy, forgiveness, acceptance, and patience. The heart is an alchemical center that transforms pain and suffering into beautiful life lessons by bringing us back into an attitude of gratitude each time we fall out of loving vibration. This chapter explores the heart space, the fourth energy center, as the bridge between your etheric and corporeal energy. Let's jump in to get to know the inner workings of this vast and airy energy center.

WHAT IS THE HEART CHAKRA?

When it comes to loving energy, there are many kinds of love: agape (selfless) love, familiar love, romantic love, love among family members, and, perhaps the most important type of love, self-love. These journeys are adventures that last a lifetime. We are always learning how to drop into more love, and we do that within the heart space, day by day. In fact, during healings, if your heart is closed, you should open this chakra first because it is a major center for spirituality and will allow the rest of your system to open up rapidly and dramatically.

Your heart chakra, or *anahata* in Sanskrit, is the fourth chakra and next up in ascending order. *Anahata* means "unhurt" or "boundless" and represents its infinite nature and resplendent resilience. This is where you access courage, peace, gratitude, coherence, and connectivity, as it's the intuitive feeling center of your chakra system. We'll talk more about heart coherence later in this chapter (page 86), but for now, understand that this center is a spiritual portal connecting you to all higher realms and the path of truest alignment. Having a strong and luminous heart field innately implies protection—your heart light will transform that which does not serve you.

The heart chakra sits in the middle of your chest, at the top of the rib cage. Anatomically, the physical organ of your heart is in the left side of your chest, whereas your chakra channel emanates directly from the center and out the back between and just under your shoulder blades. It's aligned with your cardiac plexus, a nerve bundle at the base of your heart. Your heart chakra manages your heart, lungs, thymus, shoulders, breasts, arms, and hands. It corresponds with your circulatory system, which includes your blood (blood cells, arteries, and veins), and parts of your respiratory system. Your circulatory system delivers white blood cells and antibodies to assist your body's immunity. The nerve bundles here connect to your vagus nerve, which interfaces with the heart, lungs, and digestive system. The vagus nerve is responsible for internal organ functions like vasomotor activity, heart and respiratory rate, and involuntary reflex actions (such as sneezing, coughing, and swallowing). Your heart also houses neurotransmitters that regulate other functions like alkaline balance and body temperature.

Considered both an organ and gland, the heart is fascinating, intricate, and multifunctional. It includes the thymus, a specialized organ of the immune system that makes white blood cells (T cells) to help fight infection, and is included in the heart chakra (and, more specifically, the high heart chakra covered later in this chapter, see page 86). The thymus is located halfway between the throat and heart in the upper front part of the chest.

The element associated with your anahata is air: the breeze blowing through the trees and rustling the leaves, and the molecules composing prana, which you breathe. It is the breath of life. Air is the element of intellect, stimulation, and mental energies. It provokes, stirs, and instigates, rising above its "light" connotation. This element in its purest form is steady and stable, aiding us in understanding and reasoning. The air element is denser than ether (throat) and less dense than fire (solar plexus), representing thoughts and comprehension.

The color linked with the heart space is emerald green, a frequency of nature and harmony. This vibration of green is palpable and present. It's associated with fertility, ambition, and abundance (specifically financial wealth). Energetically, this color band resonates with the vibration of love. The heart chakra can also sometimes be linked with the color pink. This is a softer aspect of the heart frequency, and we see it especially in the high heart chakra. Pink vibrates with a gentle, loving awareness. In visualization meditations, it's perfectly acceptable to invite either of these colors into the heart for amplification.

The power of the heart is vast and endless. When open, this chakra center helps with acceptance and forgiveness. When we work on inner acceptance, it helps us access unconditional love for our whole self, and it will assist in finding a path to forgiveness and peace. When this becomes a consistent conscious experience, you will no longer need to look outward for love or approval but will have cultivated them within. Letting go of the small things that hold you back will become easier, and staying present with the stream of love from Source in your heart will feel comfortable and accessible.

Your heart space is representative of the unseen realm of Source energy—of a love that connects all living things. When you are fully present and tuned in to this love, incredible miracles can begin to unfold in your life. The impossible suddenly becomes possible in new and unimaginable ways. Love has a way of lifting you up to new heights, so it's vital to nourish this energy connection. We learn best about ourselves through our ability to open up to love, and we grow strongest when that love is directed toward the self.

A Balanced Heart Chakra

A balanced heart chakra is an open and coherent heart space. The heart is able to open by clearing energy blockages through conscious intention or energy work. The power of intention is strong and works best through dedication—repeatedly returning to open up the heart, even after it has been injured or suffered great loss. This is the power of divine transformation and transfiguration—the process by which we can feel safe again in the heart. It takes commitment to truly let go of the things that no longer serve you, and courage to release and repattern unhealthy attachments and habits that keep the heart closed.

Letting go is no easy task, but you can feel the energy difference between someone who has suffered and is still carrying the heavy burden of pain compared with someone who has worked to open the heart space and welcome love back into their life. When you go through a trauma like a breakup, betrayal, or any type of abuse, it's easy to store the imprints of the negative experience in the heart. We also store old programming and conditioning here. This is where the term "heavy heart" comes from—we are creatures of habit and put things down energetically in this tender place. When you invite compassion into the heart, you can dissolve any of the hardness and heaviness, no matter how long it's been in place. An unblocked heart chakra will feel expansive, aligned, light, and free. Though hard to describe in words, you'll sense the feeling immediately and recognize it like an old friend—it's the way we each came into the world, unimaginably light.

Along with feeling luminous, a person with an open heart space appreciates things just as they are, without trying to fix them. Taking time to build a gratitude practice is one of the easiest and most common ways to create lasting heart expansion in your life. You can start by making a short list of five things a day that you feel thankful for, being careful not to repeat items from day to day. This will begin cycling gratitude energy through your heart field, magnetizing more of that same energy back to you. As you are making your list, try and drop any judgments you have of yourself and others so you can focus on the uplifting feeling of gratitude.

An open heart signifies someone who has a pleasant and friendly attitude, and takes time connecting on a deeper level with people. If your heart chakra is open, you will have an innate understanding that we are all connected, and as such, no one is truly separate from another at the level of consciousness. This understanding helps when learning how to soften judgments we hold. It also helps us express vulnerability within relationships, which brings us closer to true intimacy. This is necessary to form long-lasting bonds in all types of relationships, especially romantic ones.

An Unbalanced Heart Chakra

When your heart chakra is underperforming, it can seem as if your heart is closed off, which can have serious effects. When your heart is closed, it feels overtly guarded, as though walls have been built to keep others out. Often, this is a protective

The High Heart Chakra

Your high heart chakra is another minor chakra point located around your thymus, above the center of your chest/breastbone and below your collarbone. This energy space acts as a bridge between your heart and your soul star chakra. Located above your crown, this is your eighth chakra. The high heart is activated once your heart is opened and you are living in alignment and "heart coherence" with it. To be in heart coherence is a physiological state characterized by increased order within the mind-body connection. Heart coherence is scientifically measurable and is thought to significantly improve emotional well-being by connecting you to your heart-directed consciousness.

The more you listen to your own heart with an intention to connect to your inner guidance, the more your heart coherence grows. This helps expand an electromagnetic torus field around your heart, allowing it to swirl and grow to new levels. A zero point exists within the heart, and it's from this space you are able to access your multidimensional self and soul's purpose. There is an energy line connecting this activated chakra to the higher realms of light, which is constantly downloading information into your body to be integrated through the heart.

The more you begin to incorporate heart intelligence into your everyday life, the more this chakra will blossom and open. Your heart will deepen its connection to others and be more resilient. The connection between your heart and mind will grow, and you'll have greater compassion, empathy, and forgiveness.

mechanism that operates under the illusion it is keeping you safe, but it ends up backfiring because it isolates you from love, vulnerability, and empathy. You may feel lonely or withdrawn from others, closed off to certain people or experiences, or it might be difficult to access your emotions at all. This can happen when we are afraid to be ourselves, letting fear grow in the heart space.

You may also feel overly judgmental or as if you have disproportionately high expectations of others (or yourself). This judgment may come out as harsh criticism, self-loathing, victimization, or perfectionism. If you are demanding of others or feel the constant need to control, it is another sign you may be operating through a judgmental lens. By practicing vulnerability and working through your need to control everything around you, you'll be able to better open up your heart and slowly let more love in. One way to practice stepping into vulnerability is to simply share more of yourself and how you are feeling from an honest, self-reflective space. By allowing others to see and feel the "real you," you can build authentic relationships and expand the depths of your heart space over time.

A closed-off heart space also breeds the inability to accept things as they are. Sometimes, this is paired with denial or a complete rejection of reality. A gentle, loving awareness practice can draw you back into reality, helping you cope while you rebuild your inner resources.

Feelings of guilt, shame, and emotional pain can also contribute to a closed heart space. When we go through heartbreak, trauma, or grief, the energetic imprints of these emotions tend to get stored in the heart, increasing feelings of isolation or separation. Remember that you are never alone and all things are temporary. Working through these feelings is a pathway to healing, and these hard lessons are often an impetus for dramatic change and growth. If you are willing to surrender the stories connected to these events, your heart space will thank you by softening into a more loving state of forgiveness and acceptance. Everyone deserves to experience this flow of divinity, although we forget sometimes that it is our human birthright to continuously access this level of joy.

Physically, pay attention to signs of respiratory issues, poor circulation, or weakness in the heart space. Diseases of the heart, lungs, and lymph will affect the heart chakra. Breast or lung cancer, heart murmurs, asthma, or upper back issues can all be signs that the heart chakra has been suffering. Normally, these symptoms show up last, but by taking steps to correct the energetics of the "disease," you can help heal potential problems when they come up.

HEALING THE HEART CHAKRA

This section introduces two Reiki healing applications for the heart chakra: one for healing yourself and others, and one for distance healing. This technique builds on skills needed to get to know your own energy channel, understand how Reiki works, and explore what feels good or appropriate for the level of healing and effects desired. As you are practicing, play with what feels good, and open a dialogue when you are sharing the energy with another person so they can provide valuable feedback.

These techniques include working with the Reiki symbols, which you may or may not be accustomed to using, depending on the Reiki level to which you are attuned. There are several ways to work with the various symbols in each exercise, but because you don't need the symbols to practice Reiki, feel free to leave them out.

The following section reviews how to use Reiki for self-healing, healing of others, and distance healing and ways to use a method called the *vital charge* for clearing when you only have a short amount of time. Additionally, I go over corresponding traditional hand positions to open and unblock the heart chakra, giving you the knowledge to work on distance healing using the proxy method.

Healing the Self and Others

This section covers basic hand positions for working on your heart chakra as well as an alternate way to work with Reiki through the vital charge method. Symbols are optional for this exercise. Allow plenty of time for the treatment so it feels spacious. The suggested time limit for the traditional hand positions is about 5 minutes, whereas the time limit for the vital charge is 15 minutes. Come to a centered place beforehand through gassho or meditation so you are at your best to deliver the healing. Set an intention that the healing will work for the greatest benefit within the most beneficial timeline. This will ensure all healing is delivered exactly where it is needed and works appropriately for the highest good.

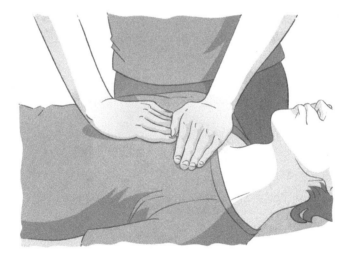

Follow these steps for this posture for self-healing:

1. Hover your hands above the center of the chest, side by side. If you and your recipient are comfortable with it, you can place your hands on the body directly under the clavicle, above the breastbone and chest.

2. Smile, relax, and intend to channel Reiki energy to this area for up to five minutes, or as long as you are intuitively guided to do so.

3. Your eyes may be open or closed, and your attention should be as it is during meditation: a soft focus on a gentle, loving awareness stream as you channel.

4. Standing behind the recipient at the head, place a hand on both upper arms at the same time. Channel for three to five minutes. This posture addresses the upper arms. As an alternate method, you may perform Reiki one arm at a time, with each hand on the upper arm and lower forearm for each side.

   The alternate vital charge position: The vital charge opens up the aura, crown, palms of the hands, and heart chakra. This is great for mini healings or moments when you don't have time for a full session.

5. Make a swiping motion with your hands three times, intending to open the aura.

6. Use both hands to open the space above your head as if you were opening a book, peeling your hands down from the top and leaving them open.

7. Channel here to your crown for up to five minutes.

8. Use both hands to swipe open your heart space. Channel here to your heart, hands hovering above the chest, palms facing toward the heart for up to five minutes.

9. Open up your palm chakras. Make a pinched fist with the fingers on the left hand and open your fingers over the right palm. Then, do the same with the opposite hand. Channel to your palms as they face each other, for up to five minutes.

10. When you are finished, come back into gassho to signal the end of the treatment. Share a moment of gratitude with your guides and Source energy for any assistance received.

When performing this treatment on someone else, the hand positions remain the same. Keep in mind that there is no need to flip someone over when performing a Reiki treatment, as the energy flows where it's needed. Unless specifically requested, the energy is just fine being channeled to the body as it faces upward.

Distance Healing

Make sure to use your HSZSN symbol if you have received it in attunement, specifying a time and place your recipient will be receiving the healing. Proceed to the next steps when you are ready.

Follow these steps for distance healing:

1. Draw the HSZSN symbol with your finger(s) directly into the space in front of you to open up the session. You may say the name of the person receiving the healing aloud (or have it written down nearby) as well as the time and place they will receive it.

If you are sending Reiki energy to yourself, you can send the energy backward or forward in time to an event or situation that needs healing. Make sure you include this in your intention when drawing the HSZSN symbol.

2. Pick a proxy for your healing. This could be a pillow, stuffed animal, a picture, or a set of crystals (one representing each of the chakras).

3. Imagine your recipient and intend that they receive the energy through the surrogate receiving on their behalf.

Hold them in your mind intentionally and focus on opening your Reiki channel as you relax and breathe.

4. Perform the hand positions over the chest and upper arms, and move along the proxy as though it were the recipient. Channel for as long as you are intuitively guided to do so.

    Bonus: Practice distance healing on yourself while holding the intention to heal a past timeline by sending energy to yourself around an event in which you experienced trauma, sadness, grief, or loss. There's no need to relive all the pain, but open yourself up to the healing available through delivering Reiki to that specific moment. Do this for 5 to 10 minutes until you feel a shift or softening.

5. Come back to gassho to signal completion and give thanks.

Mantras and Affirmations

The mantra for the heart space is "YAM." Chanting this mantra, either silently or aloud, helps build loving connection and awareness while infusing the air element into the heart chakra. Let this syllable reverberate throughout your upper chest and lower rib cage. By chanting "YAM," you will empower your heart to open. The affirmation seed for your heart chakra is "I love."

Here are some examples:

→ I am loved.

→ I choose compassion and connection.

→ My heart is open and grateful.

→ I radiate love as a beacon of light.

→ I vibrate at the frequency of love.

~~~~~~~

CHAPTER 7

THE THROAT CHAKRA

The expressive space of the throat chakra is one of truth and clarity. This tender space is a bridge that connects the high upper and lower chakras as the first "spiritual chakra." It is where we are most vulnerable and protective. The lessons here are vast and deep, and they often take a lifetime to learn. While the sacral chakra represents masculine and feminine balance, the throat space represents a balance between actions and words. Consequently, this chakra is best balanced through integrity, truth, and precise communication.

The throat chakra is meant to combine the higher learnings of intelligence you receive from your crown chakra with understanding from your heart to express your personal beliefs in a clear manner. Your truth is meant to be liberated and expressed, although authentic expression takes effort and time to master. Let's take a look at your next energy center, the throat chakra, to unlock the magic of your fifth chakra.

WHAT IS THE THROAT CHAKRA?

Deemed a "spiritual chakra," the throat is your fifth energy center signaling the ascent into your higher mind, below the third eye and the crown chakras. Here, in the form of higher consciousness, energy streams in. This energy meets with the heart's intelligence, aligning personal expression in its highest form—truth. Within the throat chakra, you can access new heights of creativity and shape your own reality through the word choices and decisions you make. The selection of words creates "spells" (that's why they call it "spelling"), and through your words, you build and shape realities. This is one reason why affirmations spoken aloud can be so powerful. Words hold the ability to realign and transform, just as actions do. Which words we use and when we use them play critical roles in our lives—the throat chakra holds so much power and strength.

Another name for the throat chakra is the Sanskrit term *vishuddha* (meaning "especially pure"). The name in its loose translation draws on the principles of clarity, truth, and alignment among thoughts, beliefs, and words. This energy center connects us to our higher divine creative expression and is concerned with all forms of communication (verbal, nonverbal, internal, and external). All these aspects contribute to healthy communication and all play a role in the development of this energy center. You'll feel more heard and understood by building your listening skills. When you are actually listening to others and to yourself, your throat chakra will thrive.

This powerful energy center is located at the center of the neck and covers the area of your ears, jaw, neck, teeth, mouth, palate, vocal cords, and trachea. It also governs the shoulders, cervical vertebrae, and upper esophagus (the rest of which is shared with the solar plexus). Considered to be the passageway between the lower body and upper body, this chakra accesses your upper spinal cord, which controls much of your body's higher functions. The thyroid and parathyroid glands are located here, which help create hormones that regulate metabolism and calcium in the body. When in balance, these glands help the cells in your body function normally, as they control various muscle, heart, bone, and digestive functions. When out of balance, you may gain or lose weight or experience an autoimmune response in the body. To keep this gland in check, simply consume regular micro-amounts of iodine, found in iodized salts, kelp, dairy, or seafood.

The element associated with your vishuddha is ether (or aether). It is the space and stillness as well as the fabric that weaves the Universe together. This is a connective element whose primary function is to more deeply connect us to our intuition, other dimensions and realms of existence, and more subtle higher-chakra energies. Ether is neither hot or cold nor wet or dry and is considered liminal, or transitional. Like space itself, it is vast, expansive, and necessary to hold all the other elements within it. The ether element here, which represents purity, is less dense than air (heart chakra) but denser than light (third eye chakra).

The color linked with the throat space is blue, a serene and stable frequency. This vibration represents healing, depth, balance, loyalty, and sincerity. It's a color that feels calming and pacifying, like tranquil cooling waters. It evokes security, trust, and authenticity, qualities that help keep the throat chakra open. Energetically, this color band resonates with the vibration of harmony.

The energy of the throat chakra plugs us into our sense of discernment and alignment, guiding us to make decisions that allow us to be fully witnessed and understood by others. You deserve to be heard and have your words and thoughts valued and appreciated. This contributes to a sense of connection, deeper love, and belonging. Your ability to verbalize and express affects your connection with your inner world, as well as how you operate and manifest in the outer world.

Your throat space is representative of the unseen realm of emotions, creativity, and balance. Be sure to observe your emotions as well as feel and express them. Curiosity about our emotions allows us to learn from them, and, most importantly, provides us access to processing through them. Your emotions are not who you are; they are temporary energies just passing through. To actually clear and release them, they need to be felt and experienced. This is how your soul grows. Suppressing emotions can end up being harmful to your well-being, so even if you need to take baby steps to acknowledge them, make sure you have an outlet of expression to ensure a healthy and open throat chakra. Next, we'll talk a little more about how these energies work and what it means to achieve balance here.

A Balanced Throat Chakra

Owning your truth is a huge throat chakra activation, which helps keep your throat open and balanced. When you were younger, it's possible that telling the truth was hard, because when you told the truth, you came up against some sort of punishment or abandonment. As you grew older, you started to recognize the value in claiming your truth and putting it "out there" for people. Sometimes this comes at a cost, but we learn to honor ourselves eventually, as remaining silent about what matters most to you is far costlier.

When your throat chakra is in balance, you'll find it takes less effort to show up fully in your interactions with people. Relationships with friends, family, coworkers, and partners become simpler because there is an ease in communicating your intentions (without needing a shockwave to get your point across). By practicing speaking your truth and consistently setting up energetic boundaries with others, you will reinforce positive nonverbal boundaries that work for you. For example, if you are a people pleaser, it might be tempting for you to give people answers that they want to hear. This type of communication can happen in a very passive way, creating guarded resentment and judgment—all feelings that get trapped in the aura and body. This often happens when we betray ourselves in order to give others what they want, and it leaves us with our needs unmet.

When you are transcending this model of behavior (a "recovering" people pleaser), you find new ways to communicate and hold your boundaries during a conversation. One way to do this is to simply let the other party know you are not available for emotional processing (also known as "dumping"). You grow by learning to accept occasionally disappointing others—and that saying "no" is perfectly acceptable. The throat chakra really draws on the power of sovereignty, which you develop from your solar plexus, and the boundary establishment you solidify in your root; the effects are amplified when these centers all open and function together. Some relationships may no longer be in heart-centered alignment with your newer, high-vibrational energies. These relationships may fall away or change as you continue to take care of your own needs and keep speaking your highest truth.

Resiliency is another facet that grows when your throat space is balanced and healthy. The ability to "let things go" is a heart-centered focus, but when we think in terms of the throat space, the ability to bounce back from a trigger or challenge can be thought of as a quality unique to the throat space. You are bigger than everyday challenges. When you have regrets, misgivings, or make false assumptions, you may feel contracted, closed off, or collapsed. If you are able to recover quickly from a disagreement and seek to recognize the lesson coming up in each moment, you can build your emotional elasticity rapidly. Instead of numbing, you can own at face value whatever comes up and let the emotions move through you. When your throat chakra is healthy, this communication dynamic feels secure, clear, and manageable.

There are some moments when you aren't able to quickly clear the emerging energies, and in those moments you may feel yourself unable to move on in a safe and healthy way. In the next section, you'll learn how to recognize signs that you may be holding on to throat chakra blocks.

An Unbalanced Throat Chakra

The throat chakra closes or becomes blocked when you limit your expression or hold back your truth in any way. There is a tendency to want to "play small," either by conforming or by minimizing the vocalization of your own needs. People do this for many reasons, especially when there is fear present. Maybe there is a fear of not fitting in or a fear of rejection. Perhaps when you were younger, your opinions weren't validated or appreciated, or maybe you suffered negative consequences for voicing your needs. There is a delicate balance between saying what you mean in a straightforward manner and being aggressively direct. Often, people who have a closed fifth energy center will focus on saying what other people want to hear instead of their authentic truth. Verbalizing your authentic opinions, needs, and desires is an important part of learning to open up the energy here and take back control, thus moving from self-abandonment to self-empowerment.

When the throat chakra is underperforming, it can be difficult to face confrontation. If you are very shy, timid, or soft-spoken, you may find it challenging to draw a line in the sand when it comes to boundaries and speaking up for yourself. Boundaries are mostly formed in the root and sacral chakras because these energy centers concern how you directly relate to others. If you have a tough time with boundaries you will want to practice verbalizing them in a safe place and create positive affirmations that reinforce your message. Remember that speaking your truth is a form of self-love.

You may be afraid to ask something of someone—for example, asking a supervisor for time off or your partner for space. In these instances, it might help to write down exactly what you need to communicate and say it out loud to yourself first as practice. You may also feel better sending a thoughtfully written message, in which you can be sure your words and message are perfectly clear. Lastly, you'll want to practice listening more in your life, which can bring a level of engagement to your conversation and provide value back in return.

There are other ways in which you may experience closures in the throat space. In a physical sense, you may suffer from vocal cord burnout, losing your voice, sore throat, stiff neck or jaw, shoulder pain, or thyroid issues. You may also experience nervousness or irritability, along with appetite fluctuations and an increased or decreased metabolic rate, which is controlled by parts of the thyroid and nervous system. If there is a general injury to the jaw, neck,

The Zeal Point Chakra

Your zeal point chakra is a minor chakra located at the base of your skull, at an approximately 45-degree, upward-facing angle. Sitting at your occipital lobe in the lower portion of your brain, this is a center for visual processing in both your waking and dream states. Some other names you may hear associated with this minor energy center are *jade pillow*, *mouth of God*, or *well of dreams*. Some chakra systems consider this a main chakra and, when it is open, clairvoyance is deeply enhanced. An activated zeal point helps bring extrasensory clarity to assist in communication.

With the throat chakra open, you can use it to balance the mind and body with your highest expression of spirituality, which enables you to share your gifts and true voice with the world. A zeal point activation may include opening up to singing, chanting, toning, or the gift of light language. Light language is a spoken form of language that many empaths experience during channeling. It includes encoded information. This chakra responds to sound, so you may want to try playing the note G# (G-sharp), its resonant frequency. In general, this will assist in opening other spiritual abilities and grounding them into an embodied state as you activate and harmonize your higher chakras.

or shoulder area, I always examine the throat chakra to determine what might be the cause. Am I authentic and manifesting integrity in my communications with others? Am I listening and taking time to process the messages I'm receiving from others to help understand them fully? By checking on these things proactively, you may help eliminate these issues in the future.

HEALING THE THROAT CHAKRA

This section introduces two Reiki healing applications for the throat chakra: one for healing yourself and others, and one for distance healing. This technique builds on skills needed to get to know your energy channel, understand how Reiki works, and explore what feels good or appropriate for the level of healing and effects desired. As you are practicing, play with what feels good, and open a dialogue when you are sharing the energy with another person so they can provide valuable feedback.

These techniques include working with the Reiki symbols, which you may or may not be accustomed to using, depending on the Reiki level to which you are attuned. There are several ways to work with the various symbols in each exercise, but because you don't need them to practice Reiki, feel free to leave them out. The following section reviews how to use Reiki for self-healing, healing of others, and distance healing.

For the first technique, I go over traditional and alternative hand placements along with symbols to use for the throat chakra to enhance emotional healing benefits. I also explain a distance healing technique using visualization. These methods have proven effective in accelerating healing while effectively saving time and energy when performing the Reiki transmission itself.

Healing the Self and Others

This exercise explains basic hand positions for working on the throat chakra as well as alternate hand positions to work with Reiki that may be more nontraditional, but are still perfectly acceptable as you build your practice with postures that work for you. Symbols are optional for this exercise, but they are suggested if they are accessible to you.

Allow plenty of time for the treatment so it feels spacious. The suggested time limit for the hand positions is 10 to 15 minutes. Come to a centered place beforehand through gassho or meditation so you are at your best to deliver the healing, and set an intention that the healing will work for the greatest benefit within the most beneficial timeline. This will ensure all healing is delivered exactly where needed and works appropriately for the highest good.

 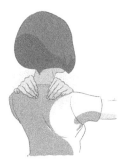

Follow these steps for this posture for self-healing:

1. Gently cup your hands on either side of the throat, making sure not to apply any pressure to the neck. The sides of your palms should be flush against the sides of the neck and the bottom of the palms should connect toward the center of the neck.

2. Smile, relax, and intend to channel Reiki energy to this area for three to five minutes, or as long as you are intuitively guided to do so. Your eyes may be open or closed and your attention should be as it is during meditation: a soft focus with a gentle, loving awareness stream as you channel.

3. Place each hand on the upper flats of the shoulders. Channel for three to five minutes. This posture addresses

the central meridian lines in the body, and you will feel energy moving all the way to your toes!

Alternate position: If this is uncomfortable or tight, you may hover your hands above your shoulders and simply intend to channel to this area.

Try using the SHK symbol. You can enter the symbol above the neck before you start the session or place it into an area needing special attention. This symbol helps release trapped and stagnant emotions that keep the chakra blocked. Draw the symbol with your fingers in the auric space and "push" it into the neck area prior to starting the Reiki transmission.

4. If you are moving on to continue to perform Reiki on the rest of the chakras, proceed by moving on to the solar plexus chakra positions.

5. When you are finished, come back into gassho to signal the end of the treatment. Share a moment of gratitude with your guides and Source energy for any assistance received.

When performing this treatment on someone else, the hand positions remain the same, but the cupping posture around the neck will change slightly. Additionally, you may also want to add the following hand position for three to five minutes.

For working on the neck on someone else:

1. The sides of your palms should be flush against the sides of the neck, with the tips of the middle fingers just touching each other as your hands connect at the front of the neck. Remember to use a light touch here with very gentle hand placement, avoiding any heavy pressure on the recipient's neck.

2. Place your hands on the top of the flats of the shoulders and channel for three to five minutes.

3. Place your hands underneath the recipient's upper back, toward the shoulder blades. Channel for three to five minutes or until complete.

Keep in mind that there is no need to flip someone over when performing a Reiki treatment, as the energy flows where it's needed. Unless specifically requested, the energy is just fine being channeled to the body as it faces upward.

Distance Healing

Make sure to use your HSZSN symbol if you have received it in attunement, specifying a time and place your recipient will be receiving the healing. Proceed to the next steps when you are ready. In this exercise, you'll be using visualization and practice with the SHK symbol.

Follow these steps for distance healing:

1. Draw the HSZSN symbol with your finger(s) directly into the space in front of you to open up the session. You may say the name of the person receiving the healing aloud (or have it written down nearby) as well as the time and place they will receive it.

   If you are sending Reiki energy to yourself, you can send the energy backward or forward in time to an event or situation that needs healing. Make sure you include this in your intention when drawing the HSZSN symbol.

2. Draw the SHK symbol with your hands and intend to place it in the recipient's aura. This symbol will activate the emotional healing and stress-relieving properties of the Reiki energy.

3. Imagine your recipient—visualize them on a small scale, shrunken down so they could fit in the palm of your hands. You may visualize a glowing SHK symbol over their body during the process.

4. Intend that they receive the energy to their throat chakra and any other area that needs healing. Hold them in your mind intentionally, and focus on opening your Reiki channel as you relax and breathe.

5. When you are finished, come back to gassho to signal completion and give thanks.

Mantras and Affirmations

The mantra for the throat space is "HAM." Chanting this mantra, silently or aloud, helps invoke serenity and openness by infusing the ether element into the throat chakra. Let this syllable reverberate throughout your upper chest and throat. By chanting "HAM," you will empower your physical and spiritual voice. The affirmation seed for your throat chakra is "I speak."

Here are some examples:

→ I speak my truth.

→ My words are beautiful.

→ My voice is my own.

→ My word is my wand; I speak and I create.

→ My voice is important.

CHAPTER 8

THE THIRD EYE CHAKRA

This chapter explores the mystical center that is your sixth chakra, known as the *third eye chakra.* This is the domain of sight—both inner and outer. When we think about sight, ideas come to mind about the eye's perception of light, color, and shape, and its ability to convey images that the mind can easily interpret. This is a function of vision—it's how we perceive the world around us. Your inner world, however, cannot be perceived by anyone else but you. Therefore, it is up to you to learn how to gain access to the landscape of the metaphysical.

This is the space in which we learn how to look beyond what is in front of us and seek deeper layers of meaning. This center informs and assimilates all the extrasensory information coming into the mind and body at any given time. Let's wade in to get to know the inner workings of this esoteric energy center.

WHAT IS THE THIRD EYE CHAKRA?

If you've ever thought about a friend only to have them reach out to you minutes later, or had a song stuck in your head only to turn on the radio and hear it playing, you're not alone. What seem like coincidences we tend to label synchronicities. These unrelated events leave us with a distinct feeling that we are receiving a spiritual message, such as "pay attention now." Spiritually, these events only have the significance we assign to them; however, as you get used to what these signs mean to you personally, you'll be on your way to opening up your psychic senses.

We are constantly flooded with nonvisual and nonverbal information, which our third eye picks up on. This subtle information is actually perceived first with our intuition, by our pineal gland, which we'll get to shortly (page 111). When this delicate and almost imperceptible information streams in, the third eye begins to interpret what it's taking in. Then we can begin to make sense of the information presented. There are several types of psychic energy that are possible for us to tap into—and some much less common types that take a bit longer to develop. Animals tend to have a very acute psychic awareness, especially cats, as they have a highly developed intuitive center. Just the way a dog can hear ranges outside the human hearing spectrum, animals can "see" alternative bandwidths of light and energy that we humans can't detect with the naked eye.

Another name for the third eye is the Sanskrit word *ajna* (meaning "summoning," "authority," "command," and "unlimited power"). The name in its loose translation draws on the principles of spiritual mastery and the power we have to see beyond the ordinary and into the extraordinary. This energy center connects us to our intuition and sixth sense and is most concerned with seeing beyond obstacles that lie before us and linking us to our visionary states. The third eye space is representative of the unseen realm of awareness and the visual realm that helps us see and understand the world.

The third eye chakra sits directly between the eye-brows at the center point of the forehead, inside the head. A pinecone-shaped pineal gland sits in the center of the brain, resting above the medulla oblongata a few inches atop the spinal column. Though the chakra location isn't exact, in general it is above and behind the sinus cavity. Sometimes the pineal gland and pituitary gland share some chakra functionality since the crown and third eye are so closely intertwined, and both glands deal with the inner workings of the brain and ocular nerves.

The element associated with ajna is light. Since this is a higher etheric chakra, it is meant to process loads of subtle information. As mentioned earlier, light contains much information, some of which we process consciously, but the majority of which is taken in as subconscious data. Photonic light energy is bright, illumi-nating, and enlightening. It has electromagnetic properties that interact with the pineal gland, allowing a person to experience light itself. Light energy helps the aura and body by raising the frequency at which we vibrate. It's also been used in chromather-apy to create certain healing effects like skin tightening (using red light), plant growth (blue light), and the promotion of calming (white light). When light energy is flowing freely in the body, we are healthier and experience deeper well-being. If the light energy is lower in the body, we may experience disease or illness. Light also facilitates communication between cells and helps repair DNA in the body, which keeps a person healthy and vibrant.

The color linked with the third eye is indigo, an intensely rich frequency. This vibration combines the serenity of deep blue with the spiritual authority of purple, a unique blend of energies. Some might perceive this as a midnight blue/purple. It's a color representing intuition, sensitivity, discovery, wisdom, and heal-ing. Energetically, this color band resonates with the vibration of focused awareness. Working with this color can help us achieve deeper levels of consciousness and, eventually, help us tap into our superconscious mind, expanding our reality infinitely.

Taking a look at which body parts are paired with the third eye, we find these located in the upper portion of the head (and some that overlap with the crown chakra). This chakra includes the eyes, pineal gland, parts of the brain and ears, hypothalamus, sinuses, and nose. The pineal gland is responsible for psychic senses and converts the light energy sensed through the optic nerve, which itself is linked to the pituitary gland (for more on this, see chapter 9, page 126) and, together, they activate functions of perception. Nerves in the pineal gland link to the limbic system, which is in charge of automatic emotions, memory, and the stress response.

The two main meridian lines, the ida and pingala, which begin in the hara (navel), actually meet here in the brain, behind the third eye. As a reminder, these represent both the left (feminine) and right (masculine) energies within. The coming together of these lines here is no coincidence—this center merges the halves into a divine whole, which initiates the opening of the third eye.

A Balanced Third Eye Chakra

The third eye chakra is a sacred space of intuition or inner knowing. For some, this chakra may remain closed for a lifetime. For those who are naturally empathic, intuitive, imaginative, and intellectual, this center will feel naturally and easily accessible. People whose third eye is open tend to be self-actualized and empowered individuals. A healthy relationship with our own consciousness is required to fully tune in to the power the third eye holds, as this space establishes a higher spiritual connection to the divine within.

An open third eye also means we are accessing our own creative wellspring. We will begin to see things as they "truly" are, which will allow a gateway to open that facilitates our stepping into our highest "creatorship" in this lifetime. Our imagination is stimulated, allowing projects and art to flow. We feel tuned in to passions of high spiritual pursuit, like meditation, Reiki, yoga, working with plant medicines, or other higher-consciousness activities. One doesn't need to be able to see auras or communicate with the Spirit realm for their third eye to be open. In fact, physically speaking, this is simply a matter of decalcifying the pineal gland.

An open and decalcified pineal gland will make a person more in tune with the natural world and the inherent messages from the Universe. Improved intuition and awareness will help us better read people, situations, and experiences so that we can more coherently direct our everyday reality. In some instances, we may feel ourselves expanding rapidly as our third eye gifts come alive. It's possible to experience enhanced psychic senses, such as clairvoyance, clairaudience, clairsentience, and precognition. These abilities expand on our natural abilities to see, hear, feel, or understand beyond normal senses.

Let's take a look at these more closely. Sight, or "voyance," deals with inner sight, and it may extend to seeing symbols or images that represent ideas communicated from Spirit guides or places that hold energy (like old homes or antiques). "Audience," or auditory abilities, may start to pick up on frequencies outside what's considered the normal human range of hearing. Sentience refers to feeling and, as this extrasensory skill set develops, we may notice ourselves picking up on other people's emotions. You'll need to spend time discerning which of these emotions belong to you and which belong to other people. Normally, the latter passes within minutes, while your own emotions are more felt for longer periods of time. Precognition, or "knowing beforehand," is a perception that occurs when you are accessing future timelines that haven't happened yet. People who experience precognition often do so through the dream state. You may be able to see details of various timelines that haven't occurred yet, like characters or settings. Pay attention to what the essence of the vision is trying to convey and use responsible discernment on relaying information if the vision involves more than yourself.

An Unbalanced Third Eye Chakra

When our third eye is underperforming, it can be difficult to access higher consciousness, intuition, and awareness. Although it's not possible to become completely disconnected from our spiritual side, sometimes it can feel that way. The divine is within each breath, so every time we inhale, we pull in more of our Spirit. When we experience grief or anguish, those are the moments that lower our vibration and create separation consciousness. You need only remember this to remain connected to Source energy running through your third eye.

We may have trouble connecting our inner vision with our outer reality when this energy center is low. Since so much of life depends on thoughts and beliefs, there may be a gap between what's happening on the inside versus the outside. Things may take longer to "manifest" in our life, and it can feel as if clarity is blurred, there is a fog of problems, or that our judgment lacks discernment. This chakra is all about mental and creative stimulation, so when this energy is diminished, new ideas and solutions have a harder time presenting themselves. We may feel cut off from our internal compass. It's so important to keep in mind that we are the creator of our reality, that we can clear the energy whenever we choose. Creative consciousness is a high frequency and will flow easily to us when our third eye energies are clear.

There may be physical symptoms present with a blocked ajna chakra. Headaches, migraines, sinus issues, earaches, tinnitus, eye problems (like vision issues or glaucoma), and seizures show up here when the energy is imbalanced. There may also be less severe signs, like nightmares or memory problems. In general, lack of vision and difficulty with planning are by far the most common physical symptoms. If there is something in our life that we are willfully ignoring, our refusal to see it can close this energy center down fast. This is why it's imperative to face our challenges in order to process and heal through them.

The Causal Chakra

The causal chakra is a minor point located at the back of the head, three to four inches outside of it. It adjoins the third eye and crown chakras and serves a similar, more amplified, spiritual function. This is technically referred to as a transpersonal chakra, as it sits outside the corporeal body. In the fictional times of Atlantis (more than 10,000 years ago), this chakra was considered one of the main chakras, and through human evolution, it eventually came to rest where it does today. As this special energy center awakens, the causal chakra becomes more in line with the rest of the chakras through the ascension column (page 138).

The energy here provides us with a deep connection to the spiritual world and divine feminine lunar energies. Associated with the moon, this chakra radiates soft white light. The moon is considered to be connected to our inner landscape of emotions, and it expands mothering energies of nurturing, allowing, and receiving. This center also allows an opening up of our natural intuitive gifts, such as telepathy and other extrasensory perception. Pay attention to how these gifts may show up subtly in your life.

The causal chakra is activated once we achieve heart coherence and all of our corporeal chakras are opened. Typically, it strengthens as we become more spiritually mature, usually after we have successfully opened the third eye chakra and feel confident in relying on our own intuition, self-reliance, and spiritual authority.

HEALING THE THIRD EYE CHAKRA

This section introduces two Reiki healing applications for the third eye chakra: one for healing yourself and others, an alternative method to access your deepest intuition, and one for distance healing. This technique builds on skills needed to get to know your energy channel, understand how Reiki works, and explore what feels good or appropriate for the level of healing and effects desired. As you are practicing, play with what feels good, and open a dialogue when you are sharing the energy with another person so they can provide valuable feedback.

These techniques include working with the Reiki symbols, which you may or may not be accustomed to using, depending on the Reiki level to which you are attuned. There are several ways to work with the various symbols in each exercise, but because you don't need the symbols to practice Reiki, feel free to leave them out. The following section reviews how to use Reiki for self-healing, healing of others, and distance healing.

I go over how to use the traditional hand placements for the third eye center for opening and unblocking. We will also take a spiritual journey to access deeper layers of the subconscious mind for healing, and work on a multidimensional visualization technique that you can use to save some time during your distance healings. As always, if you prefer, simply go over the motions for the traditional hand placements during distance healings. These alternative methods are here in case you wish to practice something different and deepen or advance your Reiki sessions.

Healing the Self and Others

This section presents basic hand positions for working on the third eye chakra as well as an alternate way to work with the Reiki through a spiritual journey. Symbols are optional for this exercise. Allow plenty of time during the treatment so it feels spacious. The suggested time limit for the traditional hand positions is

5 to 10 minutes, while the time limit for the spiritual journey is 15 to 20 minutes. Come to a centered place beforehand through gassho or meditation so you are at your best to deliver the healing and set an intention that the healing will work for the greatest benefit within the most beneficial timeline. This will ensure all healing is delivered exactly where needed and works appropriately for the highest good.

Follow these steps for this posture for self-healing:

1. Lightly place the flats of your palms over your closed eyelids. Alternatively, you may hover your hands above your closed eyes.

2. Smile, relax, and intend to channel Reiki energy to this area for up to five minutes, or as long as you are intuitively guided to do so.

3. Move your palms to your temples. Channel for three to five minutes.

4. If you are moving on to continue performing Reiki on the rest of the chakras, proceed by moving onto the throat chakra positions.

5. When you are finished, come back into gassho to signal the end of the treatment. Share a moment of gratitude with your guides, and Source energy for any assistance received.

   Note: Maintain your focus as it is during meditation: a soft focus on a gentle, loving awareness stream as you channel.

   When performing this treatment on someone else, the hand positions remain the same. It will feel best for your recipient to close their eyes, and you may either place an eye pillow on them or hover your hands over their eyes to ensure their comfort.

   An alternate practice: The spiritual journey is a meditation that allows you to travel within for answers. This is a profound way to connect to your higher levels of consciousness, and even your subconscious mind.

Follow these steps for the spiritual journey practice:

1. After your gassho, come into stillness, and open up a meditative mind-space. For the next 10 to 20 minutes, you will be on a journey.

2. Ask to connect to a guide. This may be an ethereal animal like a jaguar, hummingbird, or dolphin. Or it could be an ancestor, Spirit guide, or relative who has crossed over. Wait until you see or sense their energy arrive.

3. Imagine you are in an open hallway space together and ask them to lead you to your area of concern or issue. You may

see them leading you to a past version of yourself, a past lifetime, or the place where an injury resides in the body.

4. Ask them for assistance in your healing. Be open to any information you are receiving. Pay attention to what you are sensing, feeling, and seeing with your third eye.

5. When you feel complete with the information/healing, walk back down the hallway and come back to your Reiki positions. You may resume channeling to the third eye for about five minutes to finish this practice.

6. When you are finished, either proceed to work on the other chakras, or come back into gassho to signal the end of the treatment. Share a moment of gratitude with your guides and Source energy.

Distance Healing

Make sure to use your HSZSN symbol if you have received it in attunement, specifying a time and place your recipient will be receiving the healing. Proceed to the next steps when you are ready. This exercise explores the multidimensional self through quantum visualization.

Follow these steps for distance healing:

1. Draw the HSZSN symbol with your finger(s) directly into the space in front of you to open up the session You may say the name of the person receiving the healing aloud (or have it written down nearby) as well as the time and place they will receive it.

   If you are sending Reiki energy to yourself, you can send the energy backward or forward in time to an event or situation that needs healing. Make sure you include this in your intention when drawing the HSZSN symbol.

2. Imagine your recipient in front of you. Place the SHK symbol into their aura, if emotional healing is needed.

3. As you begin to channel, imagine yourself with multiple sets of arms, placing them on all areas of the body that need support. Because you are going quantum for this exercise, you can cover more ground in a shorter amount of time, stretching your abilities.

4. Hold your recipient in your mind intentionally, and focus on opening your Reiki channel as you relax and breathe.

5. Channel for as long as you are intuitively guided to do so, between 10 and 15 minutes.

6. Come back to gassho to signal completion and give thanks.

Mantras and Affirmations

The mantra for the third eye space is "AUM." Chanting this mantra, silently or aloud, helps build clarity and awareness by infusing the light element into the third eye chakra. Let this syllable reverberate throughout your entire head, pulling it to the space between the eyebrows. By chanting "AUM" you will help awaken your intuition and open your third eye. The affirmation seed for your third eye chakra is "I see."

Here are some examples:

→ I choose to see a higher perspective.

→ I trust my own intuitive senses.

→ My third eye is open.

→ I am clear.

→ I see and celebrate the many possible outcomes.

CHAPTER 9

THE CROWN CHAKRA

This chapter explores the crown space, the seventh chakra, which is the highest primary chakra on the body. This chakra aids in understanding, wisdom, knowing, and spirituality, and is considered etheric or divine; it helps connect us to our highest self and to Source energy.

Think of this chakra as a bridge that connects what we know in the physical world to that which is beyond. The cosmic frequencies that enter into this energy center stream in from higher transpersonal chakras and ultimately from the Universe. They help illuminate and amplify all the other chakras in the entire chakra system, which is why this chakra is considered a pinnacle. It lets the light shine through to every part of us that needs it most. Let's take a look at the crown chakra and all of its fascinating functions in greater detail.

WHAT IS THE CROWN CHAKRA?

The crown chakra is aptly named for its position at the top of the head. As the seventh chakra, this energy center acts as a bridge between the divine and physical realms and represents a union and mastery of the intellectual and spiritual domains. This chakra is usually open during childhood and then takes a lifetime to develop, since we are always learning and growing. Those who are more fully committed to a spiritual path will find that this chakra naturally stays open, as our divine energy connection is established and used regularly.

The crown signifies a synthesis of inner knowing and divine knowing. We call this *ultimate intelligence,* or *enlightenment,* when human desires, attachments, and ego concerns are transcended. Many sages and gurus from various cultures and traditions celebrated enlightenment: a type of nirvana, or samadhi, or elevated state of consciousness thought to bring relief and release from all suffering. This state of concentration is usually achieved through deep meditative practices over the course of a lifetime, ending in prolonged rapture or bliss states. Although we experience many enlightening moments during our day-to-day lives, the concept of enlightenment doesn't have quite the same meaning as it did historically. For our modern-day lives, enlightenment can simply mean self-actualization or the cultivation of one's inner purpose.

The pursuit of self-discovery, ego dissolution, and deep connection with soul are some of the most satisfying journeys in this life, and the open crown chakra is responsible for getting us there. This spiritual center governs our mental expansion as well as our mental energies, ideas, thoughts, temperance, and patience. Through this energy center, our higher-self objectives are constantly being downloaded, accessed (sometimes in unconscious ways), played out, and integrated into our being. Everything is created etherically before coming into the physical realm through the crown chakra.

Another name for the crown is the Sanskrit word *sahasrara* (meaning "thousand"). In Hinduism, each chakra is represented by a lotus, and the crown is no exception. It's represented by a thousand-petaled white lotus, which gives the crown its namesake. The name draws on the principles of spiritual mastery (along with the third eye chakra) and the power of transcendence. This energy center connects us to our own divine channel and is most concerned with the assimilation of higher knowledge. Our crown space is representative of the unseen realm of Spirit and all other realms that help us understand the world from higher perspectives. This chakra's opening plays a major role in our communion with elevated states of consciousness.

The crown chakra, sitting directly on top of the head, is sometimes described as being located within the cerebral cavity. In Hinduism, this site is referred to as *bindu* (meaning "where the soul enters the body"). In ancient texts and across cultures, the placement of this chakra sometimes is located a few inches above the head, extending outward in a field two to three feet wide.

The element associated with the crown chakra is cosmic energy. The cosmos is the fabric of the Universe that exists everywhere, across time and space and among galaxies, stars, and in every atom. The natural state of cosmic energy is pure bliss, and its presence enhances conscious expansion. Since this is a higher etheric chakra, the crown is meant to process loads of subtle information, just like the third eye. Photonic light (a type of cosmic energy) contains infinitesimal amounts of information, and this chakra is meant to synthesize all of the higher realms into physical form. There is a transcendence of thought and the ego here. In other words, the way in which we interact with the cosmos is direct and immediately enlightening. We call these packets of information received by the cosmic light "downloads."

The color linked with the crown is white light, a calming and nurturing light. This vibration also contains all the colors within it—a rainbow spectrum. It houses positive energies and can be called upon during healings to increase the effectiveness of the healing and to protect against negative energies. Energetically, this color band resonates with the vibration of pure Source consciousness. Working with this color can help us achieve deeper levels of consciousness and tap into our superconscious mind as we transcend the ego.

The body parts governed by the crown chakra include parts of the brain, brain stem, pituitary gland, cerebral cortex, and nervous system. In some systems, the bones fall under the crown as well as the skull, which of course houses the brain. We think of this area as a command center for all the major functions of the body, as well as the spiritual and emotional self. A sister gland to the pineal gland, the pituitary gland is the endocrine gland in the brain considered the master gland. It is responsible for producing human growth hormone (HGH) along with various other hormones that control the aging process and the body's inflammation response. The pituitary gland works in cooperation with the other glands to direct them and execute their functions.

The crown is responsible for transmitting chemical and electrical messages to the rest of the body, enabling one to live a normal, healthy, and active life. Let's take a closer look what it means to have a balanced crown chakra.

A Balanced Crown Chakra

We have all had that one mentor, parent, teacher, or friend that always seemed to be unfazed, patient, and wise when dealing with others. They seemed to have the answer to everything, yet they were always learning. It seems as if these individuals glowed from the inside out and radiate love and understanding. These people were no different from us, as this level of awareness and depth is available to anyone willing to put in the work. Although some are born with a general sense of peace and calm, most of us have to work at it to maintain an open and balanced crown chakra. The best way to do this is through meditation, in which we can cultivate an observer's perspective and our own sense of objective awareness, allowing ourselves to get through even the toughest of situations. Eventually we will come to a place where we have become spiritually advanced enough to start to ask, "Who is the one observing?"

Since the crown space acts as a bridge and spiritual portal between us and universal energies, when it is open, we say we have become "awakened." This can mean a number of things, but primarily it's to be spiritually aware of the Universe and all of the metaphysical connections that it holds. Once we have tapped into the oneness frequency, we start to look at all of life as being connected with a natural rhythm of cycles. We'll no longer need to filter everything through our personal lens, and we'll be better able to work with the energies of compassion and kindness because of our innate sense of belonging and unity. A simultaneous awareness exists between our individual self and everything else in the Universe. The Universe is always conspiring in our favor—we need only wake up to it to let this magic into our everyday life.

With an open crown space, our spiritual connection will be strong and we will be able to access more of our soul's higher purpose, which generates through the soul star chakra (page 129). This subtle information is passed down from the higher chakras into the crown, which continues to expand and open as it receives more instructions from our higher self and Source. We are not separate from Source, so these messages often sound as though they were coming from our own voice or the inner voice of knowing. As we start to access greater levels of true connection with our higher self, levels of our ego will dissolve and those energies that are no longer a vibrational match will gradually fall away. This realignment happens naturally and without effort. Integration happens when there are new versions of ourselves emerging, and we can let go of all the old ways of being that may have held us back in the past.

An Unbalanced Crown Chakra

When the crown is underperforming, it can be difficult to access higher consciousness and connection to inner resources. Since this chakra primarily deals with knowledge and understanding, a blocked energy center here diminishes the ability to intellectualize and reason. Physically, this may look like learning problems or judgment impairment, but it doesn't have to. It's likely more difficult to rationally discern a blockage in the crown space, as the very system that operates rationalization is the one compromised. You will need to pay attention when symptoms or signs start showing up that indicate problems, so you can unblock them.

Closures here can also manifest as an imbalance between the two sides of the brain—the left, which governs logic, and the right, which governs creativity. When one of these sides is dominant, the other side suffers. It's normal to have one side more developed than the other, but a balance of energies is what keeps the crown space open and flourishing. Imbalances here may also cause delusional or neurotic thoughts or behavior patterns. Anything irregular here can be retrained with time and effort, and through helpful healing tools like meditation, Reiki, and different types of therapy.

Common psychological symptoms may include a general lack of awareness, mindfulness, or attention. Confusion, difficulty making decisions, headaches, mental disconnection, or more serious disorders such as dementia, schizophrenia, or epilepsy, may point to an imbalance in the crown as well. Neurological disorders stem from brain dysfunction and affect the health of the mind, so they are also included in this category. Chronic fatigue, depression, or endocrine system issues may crop up. The endocrine system helps control mood, the way

The Soul Star Chakra

The soul star chakra is a chakra point that sits 6 to 12 inches above the crown space. This chakra is the eighth chakra center and is technically a transpersonal chakra, meaning it sits outside the main corporeal chakras. Once all the other chakras are open and heart coherence has been reached, this energy center becomes activated. Its direct connection with the heart space is palpable. Once we become spiritually mature, this chakra responds by blooming naturally, allowing access to our soul's original blueprint.

Through the soul's blueprint, we can rewrite timelines and contracts, and clean up or reorganize the pathways we have come to Earth to live out. Think of the soul's blueprint like a map detailing milestones and major life events, characters, and outcomes mapped out according to the soul's purpose prior to this incarnation. You may have already noticed glimmers of these destiny points playing out in your day-to-day life. When you meet someone who feels like a soul mate or who sparks déjà vu, your soul star is helping you remember who you are and where you came from.

Our divine nature continues to unfold and reveal itself through this chakra. This is a place where we get to overwrite and override past choices and lean into new timelines that integrate parts of our divine nature with our human experience. Like the causal chakra, the soul star takes time to grow and evolve.

organs work, and metabolism, so when this is "off," clear signs will usually present themselves.

Mental disorders may or may not be overtly obvious when they show up here, as symptoms are often masked or ambiguous. Narcissism and depression are examples of disorders that present in a closed crown space, and their indicators may not seem obvious at first. Narcissistic individuals exhibit behaviors like gaslighting, incongruent stories, self-centeredness, and extremely ego-centered behavior. On the other hand, depression is a mood disorder that starts with an imbalance of neurotransmitters, which can negatively affect how one thinks, feels, and acts. Depression is distinctly different from sadness or grief, which are normally only temporary emotional states. With your own or another's depression, the feelings of sadness or pain won't diminish over time (they aren't situational) and may be a result of indirect biochemical changes in the brain. I suggest that you consult with a doctor to help in understanding and diagnosing depression, rather than self-diagnosing. Since the health of the brain has an influence on all aspects of a person (mental, physical, emotional, and spiritual), keeping the brain and mind well-nourished is paramount to be able to thrive in life.

HEALING THE CROWN CHAKRA

This section introduces two Reiki healing applications for the crown chakra: one for healing yourself and others, and one for distance healing called chakra balancing. This builds on skills needed to get to know your own energy channel, understand how Reiki works, and explore what feels good or appropriate for the level of healing and effects desired. As you are practicing, play with what feels good, and open a dialogue when you are sharing the energy with another person so they can provide valuable feedback.

These techniques include working with the Reiki symbols, which you may or may not be accustomed to using, depending on the Reiki level to which you are attuned. There are several ways to work with the various symbols in each exercise, but because you don't need the symbols to practice Reiki, feel free to leave them out. The following section reviews how to use Reiki for self-healing, healing of others, and distance healing.

I go over how to use the traditional hand placements for the crown center for opening and unblocking and use the DKM or CKR symbols for this exercise. I also look more closely at a method known as chakra balancing, which can be used in person or with distance healing and takes about 20 minutes. As always, if you prefer, you can simply go over the motions for the traditional hand placements during distance healings. These alternative methods are here in case you wish to practice something different and deepen or advance your Reiki sessions.

Healing the Self and Others

This exercise covers basic hand positions for working on your crown chakra and provides an alternate way to work with the Reiki through chakra balancing. Typical Reiki sessions start at the crown and work their way down, finishing at the root, so this is where you'll begin.

The symbols to be used for this exercise are the DKM or CKR, depending on which level you are attuned for (DKM is a level 3 symbol). Allow plenty of time during the treatment so it feels spacious. The suggested time limit for the traditional hand positions is about 5 minutes, while the time limit for the chakra balancing is 15 to 20 minutes. Come to a centered place beforehand through gassho or meditation so you are at your best to deliver the healing and set an intention that the healing will work for the greatest benefit within the most beneficial timeline. This will ensure all healing is delivered exactly where needed and works appropriately for the highest good.

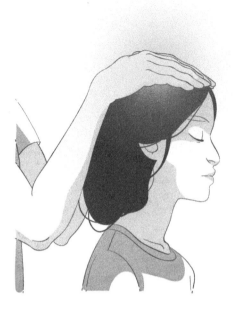

Follow these steps for this posture for self-healing:

1. Open the aura with three swipes to signal you are entering the recipient's energy field.

2. Draw the DKM and/or the CKR symbol(s) above the crown space with your fingers and gently push them into the top of the crown. The DKM symbol will help you access your divine radiance, and the CKR symbol will help you amplify the energies.

3. Signal with your hands to manually open the crown space like opening a book, if this feels natural for you. Keep your hands in your auric space for channeling.

4. Smile, relax, and intend to channel Reiki energy to the top of the head for three to five minutes, or as long as you are intuitively guided to do so. Your attention should be as it is during meditation: a soft focus on a gentle, loving aware-ness stream as you channel.

5. Move your hands around to the top back of the head, if this position is accessible, placing your hands directly on the head. Channel for three to five minutes.

6. If you are moving on to perform Reiki on the rest of the chakras, proceed to the third eye chakra positions.

7. When you are finished, come back into gassho to signal the end of the treatment. Share a moment of gratitude with your guides and Source energy for any assistance received.

When performing this treatment on someone else, the hand positions remain the same.

An alternate practice: Chakra balancing, as the term suggests, is used to balance all the chakras and is perfect if you have only 20 minutes for a full treatment session.

Follow these steps with different positions for chakra balancing, which includes channeling Reiki to two chakras, with one hand on each chakra. These steps can be used on yourself and others, as well as via distance.

1. Begin by sweeping open the auric space three times.

2. Position one: Place one hand on the crown (top of head or above head) and one hand above the root chakra. Channel here lovingly for about five minutes.

3. Position two: Place one hand on or above the third eye and one hand above or directly atop the sacral chakra area. Channel here lovingly for about five minutes.

4. Position three: Place one hand above the throat space and one hand on or above the solar plexus area. Channel here lovingly for about five minutes.

5. Position four: Place both hands on or above the heart space. Channel here lovingly for about five minutes.

6. All of your chakras are now balanced! When you are finished, come back into gassho to signal the end of the treatment. Share a moment of gratitude with your guides and Source energy.

Distance Healing

Make sure to use your HSZSN symbol, if you have received it in attunement, specifying a time and place your recipient will be receiving the healing. Proceed to the next steps when you are ready. In this exercise, we will be exploring the multidimensional self through quantum visualization.

Follow these steps for distance healing:

1. Draw the HSZSN symbol with your finger(s) directly into the space in front of you to open up the session. You may say the name of the person receiving the healing aloud (or have it written down nearby) as well as the time and place they will receive it.

   If you are sending Reiki energy to yourself, you can send the energy backward or forward in time to an event or situation that needs healing. Make sure you include this in your intention when drawing the HSZSN symbol.

2. Imagine your recipient in front of you. Place the DKM and/ or CKR symbol into their aura to increase the light energy and amplify the Reiki.

3. As you begin to channel, imagine a white light energy ball above the crown chakra of your recipient. Visualize the white ball descending through the top of the head and all the way down the spinal column.

4. Allow this white light to purify the energy center until that feels complete, while you are channeling for 5 to 10 minutes. As always, focus on opening your Reiki channel as you relax and breathe.

5. Come back to gassho to signal completion and give thanks.

Mantras and Affirmations

The mantra for the crown space is "AUM" (like the third eye) or silence. Chanting this mantra, silently or aloud, helps build focus and higher consciousness connection. If you choose to be silent for your meditation, this time is simply meant for internal reflection. Let the AUM syllable reverberate throughout your entire head, pulling it down through your chest and feeling it radiate around the top of your head. By chanting "AUM," you will empower your crown space to open and invite in divine higher energies. The affirmation seed for your crown chakra is "I know."

Here are some examples:

→ I am connected to my inner wisdom.

→ I am a unique spark of the divine.

→ I call in clarity and illumination to my being.

→ I am pure intelligence of the Universe at work.

→ I know and trust my soul's greater purpose working through me.

CHAPTER 10

THE HEALING JOURNEY CONTINUES

This healing journey is one that comes in waves, when we need it most. There will be times of contraction and expansion and times of introspection and transcendence as we rediscover and remember why we are here. Reiki, as with all healing, is heart-centered work that builds upon itself and simply takes time to learn. Don't get discouraged if you are not an expert in a day, but carve out time to dedicate to your practice and your own healing. The energy will amplify and your confidence will grow as you continue on the path, and you will pave the way for others who are open and on their own missions to spread the light in this world. You can illuminate and overcome any obstacle you face in this lifetime simply by believing it is so. This chapter looks at the future of the Reiki-chakra connection and at what steps we can take to maintain balance in our lives.

THE FUTURE OF THE REIKI-CHAKRA CONNECTION: THE ASCENSION COLUMN

Over the years, the traditional Hindu chakra system has evolved dramatically to include a Westernized version of what we receive and understand as the modern-day chakra system. We have been studying the seven primary chakras and, as humanity raises its consciousness, we are moving up in dimensional frequencies as well as in our knowledge of the chakras. The chakra system is always growing and changing. In the past 10 years or so, there have been more minor chakras discovered, especially with younger children. They all seem to have open palm chakras, ear chakras, and certain higher transpersonal chakras activated at a young age. It would seem as if natural evolution has them built for healing. These same children have intact memories from past lives and a multitude of intuitive gifts, telepathy being the most common. So what do we need to know about these changes?

My previous book, *The Complete Guide to Chakras: Activating the 12-Chakra System,* lays out the updated 12-chakra system that is based on an ascension model (the new paradigm we are in that allows us to move up in vibrational resonance as a collective). In this model, there are seven primary chakras (those included in this book) and five transpersonal chakras, which are outside the corporeal body and play a major role in how our energy operates. These chakras deal with divine, universal, cosmic, higher-self, and inner-earth energy streams and explore how they interact with our being. While this expanded view of the complete chakra system informs us on the ascension path, it's not necessary to expand to all 12 chakras to advance in the Reiki practice.

As we progressively raise our frequency, the spinal channel will continue to widen and expand. Eventually the open chakras will begin to merge together, forming a river of etheric light running up and down the spine, called the ascension column. This change begins to alter the body down to a molecular level as DNA receives repairs and upgrades. The ascension process deepens our sense of purpose and reconnection to lost parts of ourselves. Ascension is all about loving, learning our lessons, and letting go. We can't rise into higher consciousness if we are still holding on to old stories and energy. As these changes within us take place, our world is also changing. I deeply encourage each one of you to look within yourself for all guidance, as your own discernment is the most valuable tool you can connect with during this time of humanity's great awakening.

The ascension column may change the way we look at chakra healing, but it won't change the time-honored transmission of Reiki energy. In fact, the Reiki energies are receiving a boost along with all life on the planet. A greater sense of responsibility, awareness, and heart coherence are required to upgrade to these newer frequencies, and these are available to all willing hearts who continue to maintain a commitment to honoring the Reiki teachings.

MAINTAIN YOUR BALANCE

Working with this book's teachings allows you to discover that there is plenty here for you to reference, return to, and practice. Sometimes students spend years at level I and prefer to stay there. At other times, they fly by all levels within a year or two. Mastery isn't the goal—open-heartedness is. I highly recommend that you begin your Reiki practice at the crown and work your way down to finish at the root, completing your journey through all seven chakras during a healing treatment. You are encouraged to experiment with using the symbols, alternating them between different exercises, or forgoing the symbols altogether for a simple Reiki experience. All methods are perfectly acceptable and won't affect the quality of your practice.

If you set off on the journey of healing yourself, you'll eventually become comfortable working on the healing of others. This book is designed to help you in your self-healing practice, which may expand to helping heal others at any point they are feeling unbalanced, unwell, or misaligned. The important bit to remember is that you don't have to have it all figured out or be healed yourself to help heal others. By letting go of any doubts or concerns, we step aside and allow Spirit to lead us through a heart-centered path. Choosing Reiki is a life path, one of spiritual presence, vulnerability, and realness.

If you are experiencing resistance or having difficulty, remember that you can't "do it wrong." You will continue to gain so much experience as your practice matures. Remember that the chakras act simply as doorways to allow energy in and out of your system. They are fluid and approximate, so nothing should be regarded as set in stone when it comes to chakra specifics. There are always anomalies, and you'll discover your unique healing signature once you are on your way along the path, adopting what resonates and leaving the rest.

Reiki is a gentle and effective method of healing that is suitable for every age and sensitivity. The continued use of Reiki to heal the chakras and the mind-body system provides lasting transformation and healing. Reiki invokes wellness, clarity, expansion, and spiritual growth, among many other wonderful benefits. This practice helps us remember our connection to Spirit and to love. If we can allow love to work through us, we are in a surrendered flow of service and healing. We can be the light that the world needs us to be right now, and all you need to bring is your open heart.

RESOURCES

Alcantara, Margarita. Chakra Healing: *A Beginner's Guide to Self-Healing Techniques that Balance the Chakras.* Emeryville, CA: Althea Press, 2017.

A holistic beginner's guide to healing the chakras incorporating meditation, yoga, crystals, and other restorative modalities and techniques.

Hicks, Esther, and Jerry Hicks. *The Vortex: Where the Law of Attraction Assembles All Cooperative Relationships.* Carlsbad, CA: Hay House, 2008.

A channeled piece from the infamous Abraham Hicks, uncovering the powerful creative vortex that has already assembled your life and everything in it you desire. This work explores manifesting and provides practical tips for creating in all areas of your life.

Kenyon, Tom, and Wendy Kennedy. *The Great Human Potential: Walking in One's Own Light.* Montreal, Quebec: Ariane Editions, 2013.

A channeled work on the complete ascension process from two of the most well-known and respected channels we'll see in this lifetime. An accessible read on our journey as creator-beings from a Pleiadian perspective.

Pfender, April. *The Complete Guide to Chakras, Activating the 12-Chakra Energy System for Balance and Healing.* Emeryville, CA: Althea Press, 2020.

A definitive guide to the entire chakra system, including planets, deities, elements, and archetypes. This work is an ascension manual for anyone willing to go deep and heal their life across all timelines.

Pfender, April. *Essential Chakra Meditation: Awaken Your Healing Power with Meditation and Visualization*. Emeryville, CA: Althea Press, 2019.

Using intention and purpose to transform the mind and the body's vital energy centers. Also available on Audible.

St. Germain, Maureen J. *Waking Up in 5D: A Practice Guide to Multidimensional Transformation*. Rochester, VT: Bear & Company, 2017.

Insightful guidance and tools on how to shift your life into higher consciousness and how to navigate quantum reality.

Wallis, Christopher. "The Real Story on the Chakras." Hareesh. February 5, 2016. Hareesh.org/blog/2016/2/5/the-real-story -on-the-chakras.

A Yogic-Sanskrit philosopher and practitioner with thirty years of experience studying the chakras and translating ancient sacred texts gives a modern context for chakra work as it applies to traditional practices.

REFERENCES

Breit, Sigrid. "Vagus Nerve as Modulator of the Brain-Gut Axis in Psychiatric and Inflammatory Disorders." Frontiers in Psychiatry 9, no. 44 (March 13, 2018). DOI: 10.3389/fpsyt.2018.00044.

Cunha, John P. "What are the Four Types of Depression?" eMedicine Health.com. February 1, 2021. eMedicineHealth.com/ what_are_the_four_types_of_depression/article_em.htm.

Dimancea, Vlad. "Hawayo Takata – The Woman Who Brought Reiki to the Western World." ReikiScoop.com. September 2020. ReikiScoop.com/hawayo-takata-the-woman-who-brought-reiki-to-the-western-world.

Dunkin, Mary Anne. "Sperm FAQ." WebMD.com. October 24, 2020. WebMD.com/infertility-and-reproduction/guide/sperm-and -semen-faq.

Frazier, Karen. "Engaging the Flow of Reiki Through Its Three Pillars." AuthorKarenFrazier.com. September 7, 2018. AuthorKarenFrazier.com/blog/engaging-in-the-flow-of-reiki-through-its-three-pillars#.

Holland, Kimberly. "Emotional Detachment: What It Is and How to Overcome It." Healthline.com. September 3, 2019. Health line.com/health/mental-health/emotional-detachment# diagnosis.

Hughes, Aimee. "Advancing with Mantras." Yogapedia.com. December 13, 2016. Yogapedia.com/definition/8768/vam.

Janssen, Allison. "Tapping In: The Air Element." MoonlitTribe.com. September 19, 2019. MoonlitTribe.com/tapping-in-the-air-element.

Lechner, Tamara. "10 Signs of Spiritual Enlightenment & Awakening." Chopra.com. September 21, 2020. Chopra.com/ articles/10-signs-of-spiritual-enlightenment-awakening.

McCraty, Rollin, PhD. "The Heart-Brain Connection." HeartMath.com. January 2018. HeartMath.com/science.

MedlinePlus. "Adrenal Gland Disorders." U.S. National Library of Medicine. Accessed April 27, 2021. MedlinePlus.gov/adrenal glanddisorders.html.

Myota, Peig. "Light Therapy, Healing and the Power of Love." NaturalMKE.com. March 31, 2021. NaturalMKEcom/2021/03/31/ 351897/light-therapy-healing-and-the-power-of-love.

Nuur, Deganit. "The Four Divine Energy Types." Goop.com. May 2021.

Goop.com/wellness/spirituality/balancing-your-feminine-and -masculine-energies/#:~:text=We%20call%20it%20%E2% 80%9C

Greater%20Yin,when%20we%20feel%20harmonious%20within.

INDEX

ACKNOWLEDGMENTS

I'd like to extend infinite gratitude to the eternal song of my heart, my beloved heartpartner, Dr. William Coward. Thank you for inspiring, encouraging, and loving me. Thank you for believing in this important work. It is the greatest gift to get to play with you throughout this life and all our cosmic timelines throughout eternity. I love you endlessly.

Special acknowledgments to my Maui *ohana*, and multidimensional jewels: Sydney Campos, Becki Weeks, Frank Kanekoa, Carson Barnes, Athena and Charlie & the Spaship, Gina *Radiant Essence* Badamo.

And to my sisters who will always be at the core of my heart as we walk this path together: Torri Fitzgerald, Natalie Valle, Ashley Frey, Tiffany P. Schmidt, Kim Dudine, Sky Hardison, Sabrina Hill, Chelsea Didier, Heaven Hurley, Val Sepulveda, Kristen O'Connell, and Jane Trieu.

Thank you, I love you.

ABOUT THE AUTHOR

APRIL PFENDER is the founder of Golden Light Alchemy, a healing company that combines her years of trauma-informed healing with Reiki, and other various healing modalities. April is a Reiki Master Teacher, quantum and sound healer, and meditation instructor who has been studying and writing about the chakras for years.

April is a daughter, mother, lover, healer, wayshower, and teacher to many. She currently resides in Maui, Hawaii, with her beloved French bulldog Skyla where she hosts virtual and in-person training classes as well as retreats.